IN BLACK ROCK

REIKO YAMAMOTO

Can sake improve your health and relationships?

In Black Rock

Published by Cyberhedz Media LLC

ISBN: 9798630109842

Cover design by Reiko Yamamoto

Dedication

This book is dedicated to the people who helped me make this book a reality and who inspired me.

Acknowledgments

A lot of people believe that there is nothing you can do alone, and you always need the support of someone else around you to help you achieve something. Similar is the case with me. I have a lot of people who played a part in assisting me with the completion of this book and with this section I would like to extend my gratitude towards those who inspired me to write this book.

About the Author

Reiko Yamamoto is an avid fan of sake who has delved deep into the world of the distinctive rice wine and come out with a comprehensive guide about it. The writer has deep knowledge in history of the drink and has always wanted the world to know what goes into making it. With years of experience in the industry and with a comprehensive library of knowledge, there really is no better person to spread knowledge about sake.

The author provides all of the information about sake, from cultivating the rice to processing, and the people that are involved. The growing popularity in the United States, Europe, and the Asia Pacific driving its consumption. This book is the complete guide of all things about sake.

Preface

In recent years different cultures of the world have become more accessible via the Internet, then comes new inventions like the chase game. The direct result of this is a global affinity of sake, a Japnese rice wine. It has become a world phenomenon, and they have come up with their version of flavor and food pairing.

The term 'sake (saké)' is widely known around the world as 'Rice Wine.' Still, not all are aware of how this prestigious liquor of Japanese came about, where it originated from, what led to its growth, where it stands currently. Now you'll have a chance to be part of this new wave of sake within the setting of Black Rock City.

Get ready to savor every sip of sake, and don't be surprised if you are left convinced to allow its various flavors to grace your taste buds after reading this book!

Contents

Chapter 1
What is Sake?

I run my sake bar in Black Rock City

On Monday, August 26, 2019, around 6 P.M., I found myself mixing a concoction of a sake cocktail shortly after landing in Black Rock City (BRC). I remember the temperature clearly, it was a little over 100°F. Of course, my excitement and anticipation of what waited for me had only increased the temperature a little more for my jittery nerves. Eizo, a Japanese sushi maestro, and chef in his 30s, was displaying his maestro skills beside me on a 10 ft. long counter that offered shrimp nigiri sushi to all the half-naked burners.

Now, you must be wondering who I am and who these burners are. Well, allow me to quickly introduce myself to you. My name is Reiko Yamamoto. I knew little about sake, let alone how to infuse it seamlessly into other drinks to form a concoction that would be a crowd-pleaser. Here I was, at the once-a-year event known as 'Burning Man' during the Labor Day weekend. Let me shed some more insight into Burning Man. It is an annual event where a crowd of 80,000 is expected.

People from all around the world gather to attend this 10-day event at the one-and-only city of Black Rock. The city is hosted temporarily in the desert of Northwest Nevada, roughly located about 100 miles northeast of Reno. There is no internet and no proper infrastructure present. Camps are loitered all around, dry air prevails, and music is played at full volume in the bustling annual affair organized by both local and international patrons.

An array of sake bottles occupied the counter as I busied myself behind, my eyes would take in Eizo's sight. The man was absolutely lost in the world before us. He was engrossed in flipping sushi and sliding them across the table to the patrons without their bras on. What amused me the most was that each time I looked at Eizo interacting with the people, I watched in awe because of the very fact that none of them spoke or understood Japanese. Eizo, on the other hand, communicated in his native language. For a peculiar reason, both Eizo and his patrons seemed to have established a sense of understanding. I was reminded of the scene from Blade Runner, where Harrison Ford had placed an order for a bowl of noodles at the Japanese cart. He had spoken to the chef in English, and the chef had responded in Japanese. Still, Harrison Ford had managed to get his desired meal in the noir looking in the city of Los Angeles. It was the same in this instance. BRC is noir, except the fact that instead of rain, there was dust.

When I first saw the opening of the movie and how Eizo was interacting his customer in front of him, I felt strange as I understood both sides of the world. Such as why a chef who responded in Japanese while understanding some simple English. It is the cultural and grammatical difference that makes it next to impossible for any Japanese native to compose an English sentence. I think this goes the other way around, too. For this instance, I begin my journey of sake with an event called Burning Man.

You must be wondering why the event is named Burning Man? Well, the event has more to it than just art, entertainment, music, food, and drinks. In this event, the participants are known as burners because of burning dummy men, temples, and other structures heaved on a nightly basis. If this gives you the impression that the event is hazardous, then you are mistaken. Strict rules and regulations are imposed, the event is patrolled, and safety kits and aid are available throughout. Furthermore, Burning Man has 10 principles that are always adhered to. One of these is Decommodification.

Decommodification: In order to preserve the spirit of gifting, our community seeks to create social environments that are unmediated by commercial sponsorships, transactions, or advertising. We stand ready to protect our culture from such exploitation. We resist the substitution of consumption for participatory experience. -Larry Harvey, co-founder.

The 10 principle explains the ideology behind the event and the decommodification principle is to prohibit the attendees from making money out of it. It is not a profit-oriented event. There are camps throughout the city. Each camp is themed and formed by the camp organizers, who then submit their proposal when approved by the non-profit Burning Man Organization. The participant needs to purchase their own ticket which ranges from $225 to $1400 per person. Despite the price difference, all tickets are the same. Apart from paying the ticket, the camp members need to pay a camp fee as well. A camp that is well-founded or has the best theme can attract more burners and is rewarded with more ticket allocations next year by the Burning Man Organization. Most of the camps offer a variety of alcoholic drinks at their bar at no additional cost to their patrons, but they are unable to accomplish the very idea behind the event. They fail to attract burners to their bars due to the high temperature and dryness of Black Rock. After all, Black Rock is located in the desert on a dried-up lake bed. The burners would reluctantly opt-out of any alcoholic drinks and opt for water instead.

I got the role of the lead bartender at a sake bar in Camp Synthesis during 2019's Burning Man, offering sake and sushi right beside a D.J. named Brian who played synthesized music and is organized by David. Out of the 10 members in the camp, most of them were white and Asian. Most of us were from Silicon Valley, working at high-tech companies, excluding Ryan and Eizo. Ryan was a sound engineer from Las Vegas who had scored a low-income discount ticket at $225. Compared to the Silicon Valley Standard, anybody else can be qualified to this category but, then he was the only one able to afford an RV with an air conditioner out of 10 members.

The burners were less interested in alcoholic drinks and were mostly there for Eizo's tantalizing sushi artwork. There were too many bars offering drinks, it was like an exhibition of alcohol. Things only started to change after I joined. The people around me, including the camp members, started to grow eager for the sake cocktails that I was shaking.

More and more people started to crave my drinks. By the third day, people had started to only come for a drink. They would chime happily,

"We've heard this camp serves the best sake cocktail."

For some reason, most of them appeared as a couple and became more intimate after a couple of sake cocktails. With that, the fate of our camp changed. The need to lure burners into our camp diminished as my sake bar became bait. Now there is a reason I was able to develop an ever-growing fandom for my sake bar that seemed to be improving my patrons' relationships.

According to the 2018 BRC census, the participants were mostly college graduates, around 35 years old, white, affluent, heterosexual, monogamous, in a relationship, or married. Also, over 60 percent of them were there to feel a sense of belonging. I saw there was a fact in the firsthand. Unlike the majority, I'm Asian and had a different motivation to be there. It is a journey in itself that goes way back, even before I signed up for the Burning Man. My journey to the sake bar started when I had a job as a UX Designer for my former employer, a Fortune 10 company in San Francisco. In the summer of 2018, I had to visit Japan for 14 days, which was my paid time off.

My journey to the sake bar started when I had a job as a UX Designer for my former employer, a Fortune 10 company in San Francisco. In the summer of 2018, I had to visit Japan for 14 days, which was my paid time off.

The reason behind my visit was to head back to Osaka, my hometown, to invest in a property at a cheaper rate compared to San Francisco. In San Francisco, I could not even buy a parking space at that price, and it was plan B for my retirement.

I was unprepared for the shocking reveal upon arriving back in San Francisco. I had returned to an unexpected termination. I was amongst the unlucky lot who were retrenched. I was in the IT department and designing the user experience of the applications on a healthcare data platform. This IT department wasn't returning much investment. When the company's main business, such as pharmaceutical distribution went south, they quickly assessed some money saving strategies.

I could not sit idle or mourn over my lost job. Thus, I began a strenuous and mundane process of finding a new job. The only thing different this time around for me was an unexpected and unwritten requirement. Almost all employers sought at least one volunteer experience from their prospective employees to ensure their ability to participate in society. This was the beginning of an unexpected journey for me. After going through endless job requirements, I started to search for different volunteering experiences, until Burning Man caught my attention.

Having spent more than two decades in San Francisco, I occasionally hear of Burning Man. I never felt intrigued enough to participate until I deliberated over the option, "It's only a once a year commitment", or so I thought. Usually, local event volunteering comes almost monthly cadence, and I decided to sign up for it. After I completed a few volunteering duties and listed them on my LinkedIn page, I managed to secure a new job at a startup venture shortly after Labor Day. At my new employment is where I discovered new colleagues that were always talking about Burning Man.

This all riled me to be more interested in the event, and it got me asking, "How do I participate in it?"

I was told the process was rather easy, "You can simply participate at a theme camp. They always have tickets."

"Great, how much would that cost?"

I was clueless about how to purchase the event ticket, and my colleagues seemed to know all the details by heart, and their answers came rapidly.

"Oh, the camps will actually charge a membership fee. And depending on the rapport of the camp, it can range anywhere from $0 to $10,000."

They instructed me to create my profile on burningman.org, and so I sent out my inquiries for the Burning Man Theme Camps via the website. The decision was made in a spur of the moment, and I ended up participating in Camp Synthesis since they had no membership fee. I offered my services to be a sake bartender. This was enough to get me in, except there was a drastic issue on my behalf… I knew nothing about sake.

One would imagine that hailing from Japan, maybe I would have basic knowledge of sake, but the truth is, not many Japanese people nowadays consume sake and know nothing about it. To be a bartender, I had to know my drink better than I knew the back of my hand. Before my panic could settle in me, my mind came up with a quick solution: I could simply seek a crash course to understand the drink and its contents better, and how to bring about the drink in a better light. It seemed like fate had already planned something for me, since my new office was situated in Berkeley, CA, near the UC Berkeley campus. Near my office, there happened to be a modest Japanese restaurant and shop named Tamon. To better grasp the idea behind Japanese cuisine, I strolled into the store for lunch one afternoon, unbeknownst to what more was in store for me. Tamon specializes in Japanese rice balls, also known as 'onigiri.' Having tried them for myself, I can vouch that Tamon makes the best onigiri.

As I placed my order for a couple of onigiris, I picked up one of the classified ads lying idle in the shop. There was a Help Wanted ad for one of Japan's largest sake breweries, and its subsidiary was looking for a Sake Testing Room Attendant, and I immediately applied for the job. I was hired! This was where I was exposed to a world of sake, the different kinds of sake, the process of making it, and so much more. There is more to sake than what meets the eye. Through this book, I would like to share all that I learned from my job at the tasting room and what ignited a love for sake within me. Let's take a look at the basics.

Deep dive into sake

After I passed the online bartending exam, I was placed in the part-time shift, with six other part-time tasting room attendants and two full-time managers. Nonetheless, I had to conduct five sessions over the course of Saturday or Sunday, sometimes both within my seven-hour shift for each day. Each session revolved around sake and I conducted a basic introductory session. The limited-time restrained me from sharing as much information about sake as possible. If I have ever been granted a little more time, then this was all that I would have shared.

As many of us may know, sake is a Japanese alcoholic drink made from rice. To simply stated it, sake is rice wine. Commonly, sake is also referred to as Nihonshu in Japanese, which translates into "Japanese Alcohol" in English. If you look closely at a sake bottle in the U.S.A. that was imported from Japan, you will notice the label says Seishu rather than Nihonshu. Seishu means clear alcohol and is imposed by Japan's Liquor Laws, albeit Seishu is not commonly used in conversations in Japan, hence the term Nihonshu, because who would say clear alcohol and not Japanese Alcohol? So there is certainly some confusion here. Seishu is a term used to classify alcohol in Japan for the purpose of labeling bottles. But then all sake labeled as Seishu is not always classified as rice wine in the U.S.

Seishu is derived from the word sake (which means alcoholic beverage), which means: to be filtered and the liquid is clear. So Seishu means a clear, alcoholic rice wine.

These milky-colored drinks are usually identified as unfiltered sake containing rice particles, known as Nigori. Nigori means Cloudy in English, however, it is classified as Seishu. The process of making Nigori begins by using a broad mesh during the pressing stage. This allows for the fine rice particles to pass through while retaining the cloudy texture of the rice. Thus, Nigori can also fall under the Seishu category in Japan by law. Sake that is sold in the U.S. regulates a limited percentage of alcohol up to 22%. But usually, sake contains about 15% to meet the majority of the market. For the drink to be classified as Seishu as per the Japanese Liquor Law, it would mean for the beverage to have a percentage of spirit below 22%.

In Japan, they also regulate the labeling system. Junmai, which means pure Japanese rice, is made only from the four raw materials comprising Rice, Water, Koji, and Yeast. Surely, other ingredients are also allowed to be used in the making of Seishu. Some of these include the brewer's alcohol; thus, the label doesn't have Junmai.

The total weight of added ingredients should not exceed 50% of that as compared to the weight of the Junmai, and the Kome-Koji or rice-based koji being used. In the U.S., this alcohol added style is not classified as rice wine but hard liquor. The Japanese Liquor Law ensures that each ingredient, procedure, and process is carefully monitored and regulated so that the percentage of Seishu stays within the acceptable range of 12-20%.

Key terms and process of making sake

Now sake may sound as if it is monotonous and one sort of a drink, but in truth, it varies drastically. Each step and ingredient plays a vital role in the types of sake being produced. This means a customer will be spoilt with choices. However, these choices can be overwhelming for a newbie who wishes to discover a type of sake that befits their wants. This is where I step in. With this book, the need to be a sake samurai diminishes as the book is here to serve as a Holy Grail for Sakes out there. To get you started, I have mentioned the basic terms used in the production of sake to help you get through the basic process.

To begin with, the process of brewing sake is extensive and can be complicated. There are over 10 steps involved: Rice Milling, Rice Washing, Rice Soaking, Rice Steaming, Koji Making, Moto/Shubo (Fermentation), Moromi (the mashing), Pressing, Filtration, Pasteurization, Storage, and Bottling. Each step is highly crucial to the making of sake. One trivial mistake or negligence could unbalance the taste and quality of the sake.

Previously, I mentioned that sake with no distilled alcohol added is Junmai and is made only from rice, water, koji, and yeast. Meanwhile Seishu (sake) can contain distilled alcohol, a premium sake with distilled alcohol is labeled as Honjozo. Both Junmai and Honjozo are labeled as Seishu in Japan. I will now elaborate on the need for using only Junmai sake to help you understand better its significance and importance in brewing a high-quality sake.

Junmai

Junmai means pure rice in English. The word refers to a type of sake brewed without any added distilled alcohol. The proper way to brew Junmai is to adhere to the usage of rice, water, yeast, and koji. Additives like sugar and alcohol are not used. If a bottle of Seishu does not have the word Junmai (純米) written on it in Japanese, the beverage would be containing other brewers and additives. This makes Junmai sound like an exemplary drink, right? Well, it is pure, natural, and has no preservatives at all.

Different forms of sake can be good, and at times, better than Junmai. No one sake is inferior to the other. It's just that these trivial details of ingredients and processes alter the taste, and each drinker has its own liking. So this way, sake can cater to the needs of all taste buds. Most professional and experienced brewers add distilled brewing alcohol too to enhance the flavor and aroma of the drink, altering the texture too amidst the process. This way, some sake has a stronger taste, and some can be easy to drink.

Polishing

This is the first step to making sake. Often polishing is also referred to as milling and is important in shaping the structure of the rice grain used. Each and every rice grain is polished to perfection, meaning buffing off its bran as the outer layers of a rice grain are rich in fat, mineral, and protein. It is the inner component that is necessary to sake-making. That is, where the starch is. Buffing machines are used in this procedure and can transform brown rice into white rice seamlessly. Naturally, if you are transforming brown rice into a polished and finer seimai or polished rice in English, it would mean polishing 10% of the rice bran.

Another thing to take note of is the percentage of rice polished. The more polished it is, the finer and richer the taste of the sake would be. The outer layer of a rice grain is rich in protein, fats, and minerals when it comes down to sake. These elements are considered as miscellaneous, unwanted teats, and are called Zatsumi by bowers. The over-polishing rice would result in sweet, sour, salty, and fruity Sake since some of the starch can be polished off too.

It is advisable for a rich sake to be brewed from 50-70%

polished rice. This would mean that 30-50% of the outer layer of the rice is buffed off. The percentage of the polishing process regulates the classification level. Although, as mentioned above, a higher percentage of polished rice does not imply that the sake will be good.

Again, this depends on the drinker's taste bud. Some people prefer their local, cheap brew, and some have a liking for something more fine and refined. This is the beauty of sake, as the different varieties available on the market cater to every need. Once this is taken care of, the brewers then can move on to the next steps. But I will talk about the remaining details later in the book.

By the end of the book, I guarantee that you will come to see for yourself just why sake is carved around the globe now. The raw materials used undergo special speculation, and a thorough process before it can be bottled. One key term amidst the process is known as 'straining.' This step varies from filtration, which determines if a sake is filtered or unfiltered. Straining separates the rice particles (Sake Kasu) from the liquid (Seishu). I can understand if the words and information seem to be a lot to wrap your mind around. I will take you along on my journey that helped me discover sake so that you too, can understand the science behind this drink better.

Apart from Junmai sake, another common type of sake

available is the Honzo-Jo. This is not as pure as Junmai sake because, in this version, brewers freely add extra additives such as more contents of alcohol. To help you understand the variants better, I have attached a graph with the types of sake, both pure and impure, along with their percentages of alcohol.

One thing that distilled alcohol does is that it refines the overall sake texture. The liquid becomes easier to be lighter and dry. As a result, such a sake becomes easier to drink in comparison with Junmai sake. In some cases, the amount of distilled alcohol to be added is pre-set, for example, in Ginjo sake. The limit is set at 10% of the white rice weight. The aim is to have an effect on the quality rather than the overall quantity of the drink.

One such effect the distilled alcohol has is the fragrance it contributes. Some components of the Ginjo sake are soluble in alcohol. Hence by mixing the distilled alcohol, the scent these components have in Ginjo sake is retained even with the addition of distilled alcohol. The distilled alcohol ensures an even quality of sake throughout. Since Junmai sake is not dependent on distilled alcohol, its quality is drastically affected by the kind of rice used and the weather. While distilled alcohol affects the overall quality of the sake, consumers tend to get inclined toward a stable taste. The addition of this brewed alcohol is a common practice by larger breweries.

In 2019, 60% of sake produced in Japan (seemingly in bulk) is Futsu-Shu or no name sake in English. The rice is polished to about 70%, which means only 30% of the outer layer is removed, giving the sake a texture, rich in protein, minerals, and fats. Furthermore, an additional 20% Jozo-Alcohol is added, which weighs the same as the 20-30% weight removed from the rice grain.

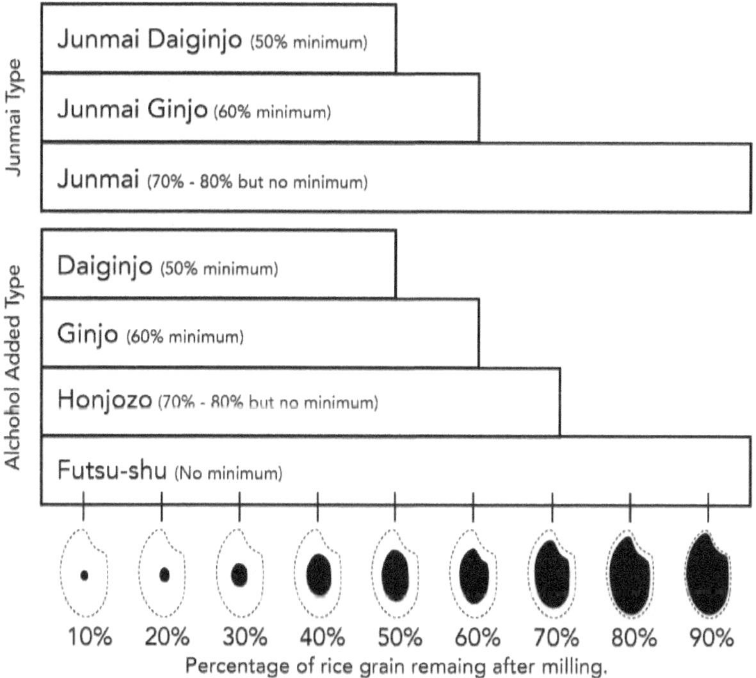

I am certain you can now calculate the percentage and weight of sake yourself and test your basic knowledge when you spot a sake bottle on your next trip to a store. Now that you are familiar with the terms polishing and Junmai, let's explore the rest of the making of sake in-depth, shall we? I guarantee you, my journey will excite you just as much as it excited me. We will begin by differentiating the vast range of Sakes available to help you find something of your preference.

Chapter 2
The Different Types of Sake

What type of sake to bring to BRC?
Before I begin talking about the different types of sake, let me share my experience on how I came about selecting the type of sake to bring with me to the Burning Man.

This decision process of picking the sake came about after I had secured my gig at the tasting room. At this point, I still had little to no knowledge about sake, let alone it's market. It was three days before the event, I drove to the tasting room from my office, where I met with a couple of full-time employees who seemed to have changed my perspective about sake entirely. How? You will learn soon.

One of the managers of the tasting room had appeared on the New York Times column for her role and had given over a couple of decades of her service to the tasting room. She seemed intrigued by my wondering and mentioned how at this time of year, a group of people stops by to purchase a couple of boxes of 18 liters sake en route to Burning Man.

As I have mentioned in the first chapter, Junmai sake is made from rice, water, koji, and yeast, or to simply put it as Rice Wine in English. The tasting room had a showroom and a museum, where I was gazing at over 30 types of Junmai they had. Of course, if I had an unlimited budget, I'd choose Daiginjo sake that tastes fruity with floral aromas. It seems to me most of the patrons that came to the tasting room agree with me about my choice, but then if I were to bring something else, I doubted if people without any prior exposure to dry sake can even swallow it.

At the Berkeley brewery, there was a type of Junmai that is made of 70% of polished Calrose rice, which is native to California. Calrose rice is harvested in Sacramento Valley and brewed locally in Berkeley, California. There are many breweries present in California because of this, California harvested Calrose rice and also Sierra Nevada water.

I bet on the possibility with David, the theme camp organizer, if he can find my ticket, I will buy a supply for the sake bar. What I didn't know about the camp was that it was their inaugural year and got no tickets allocated by the Burning Man organization. Unexpectedly, he found one for me, and so I needed to rely on my employee discount to score a few cases of sake.

There was not much time left on my watch as the event was in two days' time as I had purchased the ticket at the very last minute. The whole ordeal I had to go through to purchase the tickets for Burning Man event was a journey I was unprepared for. You see, while I had to register to buy the event ticket, I also had to sign up for the theme camp as the lead bartender, as a backup plan to acquire the ticket through their network, unaware of the cost and the fact that the tickets sold off like hot cakes within the first few minutes of the first day of sales. There were no extra tickets available from the main sale. Furthermore, I discovered that the gin and automation entry ticket costs $425. I then waited for OMG sale at $550 per person. Much to my dismay, I had missed my opportunity to get an entry ticket. The event was fairly popular, after all, with patrons flying from all over the globe.

I mean, what more can one ask for when they get unlimited access to alcohol and watch the structures burn like the fireworks at a Disneyland Parade. Fascinating to see instead of Mickey Mouse running around the castle, the Burning Man structures are crafted so that they put up an act of turning to ashes, which is unexpectedly entertaining.

The tickets for Burning Man were available on their official website. Nonetheless, as fate may have it, I was contacted by Teresa, a member of the Camp Synthesis whom I had never met before in my life. I was left baffled when she told me that one of her Facebook friends was offering to sell off a spare ticket at half the price. This was an unusual occurrence. By the way, most of the theme camps have a Facebook group for posting any information on their pages. Commonly, people were willing to pay tenfold for the Burning Man ticket due to its popularity. For me, there came the opportunity of purchasing the ticket for half the price. I was all the more interested, especially after knowing that the Burning Man organizers were always closely regulating the sale of tickets to make sure that people are not selling them more than the face value.

Teresa, her friend Tim, and I got chatting via Facebook Messenger. She was quick to share how she and her friend were selling the ticket. Tim, the old venue organizer of a theme camp, and Teresa, both lived in San Carlos in Silicon Valley and offered me to join them at the local Pizza restaurant bar since this would be my first time participating in the Burning Man event. Unable to refrain, I questioned her about the ticket price since I knew the range was from $225 to $1400.

"Well, you can get it for $700," Teresa said.

I deliberated. Tim was selling a FOMO ticket, also known as a pre-sale ticket, that is usually more expensive than the main tickets. I quickly added $100 for a parking permit to drive a vehicle in, plus food and beverages cost could be another $500-$1,000, only to know that it would still cost me a good fortune. I hesitated before asking if there were any other tickets available, as the FOMO ticket was costing a lot. Much to my surprise, she turned out to be quite understanding of my predicament.

"Is there any additional cost apart from adding the vehicle and food and beverages cost?"

"No, not at all."

"Okay, I'll buy it. Where can I get them from?"

This time, I was the one who was ecstatic. I had a chance to get a ticket to Burning Man.

"The sale takes place uphill in San Carlos."

As told, once I drove to the venue in a hart of Silicon Valley from Berkeley after work, I was surprised to see Tim's Burning Man group was very much like everyday guys and gals. Some of them had to sell the tickets due to their partners backing out at the last minute or unforeseen circumstances, either. The ones like me, who were able to get a ticket, were beaming. I had bought a ticket from a guy, Tim. He had initially bought the ticket for his brother, but for reasons, his brother was uncertain about participating in Burning Man. I guess one man's loss is truly another one's treasure. Tim's brother's reluctance was becoming my treasure.

After purchasing my ticket, a group of Tim's party was there at the bar and having the micro crafted pints of draft beer meanwhile their kids were running around.

As per the group, they would regularly meet at the bar once a month. The longer I chat with them, I discovered that they've participated in Burning Man event every year for over 10 years. Together Tim and his circle of friends seemed to know their drinks inside and out. They can talk about any episodes associated with a type of beer they said they like, and at one point, the bar stopped carrying and then begged them to bring it back on tap. This left me to question myself, "Why did no one I knew ever have knowledge of or interest in sake?"

Sure, there were a couple of older men, inclusive of my dad, who would indulge in sake. That was all to it. As the generations changed and time passed, no one, not even someone from my own generation, seemed to know anything about sake.

Observing Teresa, Tim, and his group, I realized this was an aspect that I needed to dig in. I needed to know more about sake, much like the two of them knew beer. Observing Tim, I came across another realization. The reason they knew so much about beer was the quality. Usually, 80% of sake drinkers are not interested in knowing about the drink due to the low quality being produced. Even the ones being produced in Japan, it seems that the brewers are only making it for the mass market. It may be linked to the Japanese income being stagnated some time back due to the real estate bubble crisis around the year 2000. Way before the bubble, another factor affecting the production of sake is WWII. After the war, sake infused with the distilled spirit was being produced due to the rice shortage.

Although, Sake's taste can be justified based on the

quality and type of rice grain used. Unlike grape wine, sake is not classified based on the kind of rice used, like Merlot and Chardonnay while sake's grade and flavor vary based on the rice used. Sounds confusing, right? Saying that we want a sake made from famed 100% Yamadanishiki rice, doesn't mean the same as asking for a Chardonnay.

I had received my ticket on Thursday night, which meant I had only the weekend to prepare and wrap up my work. Moving forward, I finally made my way to BRC by driving my car. From there I was on a rented bicycle on Monday in Playa. The BRC was erected on the Playa, as the organizers called it, which is a Spanish word translating to a beach. The only irony was that this beach was dried up. The plain desert was arid, and dust was flying everywhere. After all, the temporary metropolis was standing on a once-upon-a-time lake. The harsh weather made me carry a gallon of water with me everywhere. Cycling my way around only made me sweat like never before.

People who had rented RVs were paying over 10 grand a week. Some of them even had to pay as much as $5,000 and up to rent a van to bring their pods to BRC.

This was one of the many reasons why I was cruising on my bike during the event. I had no RV or exclusive council membership to reap the benefits of staying at the venture club pro. The council members and a few others had pods, which were temporary living structures constructed out of a semi-wood material.

Before coming here, I had asked David about the sort of camping gear I should bring as I would need a tent to sleep in. To my delight, he was kind enough to render me his spare tent. I did not have many belongings to carry, but having to sleep in the tent each night made me realize it was in vain. The flimsy material sheltering me was only a thin barrier between me and the open sky. The heat of the desert was able to penetrate through the material of the tent and pierce through our skin.

It was in vain to try and gather some sleep in the daytime. At night, the weather would turn chilly and if I tried to fall asleep, I still wouldn't be able to get sound sleep. This had me waking up around six o'clock and leaving the tent to escape the heat. By 9 am, I would just be cruising around BRC. During my cruising, I came across a canopy that have caught my attention. There was a guy sitting on a chair next to a foldable table, and the signage next to him read Sake and Tea.

It was a small themed camp, like others around there. This camp was called "Through the Looking Glass." There were a couple of people standing in the canopy and dipping paintbrushes in water ink before writing what I deemed to be Chinese calligraphy. It was a mesmerizing sight to watch.

I found myself to have stopped there. As the three people were conversing among themselves, I realized they had a rather strong British accent and introduced themselves with their Playa names. The BRC was erected on a desert plain as the Burning Man organizers had rented the federal property for this, calling it Playa. This allowed the participants to create their playa names, behind which I understood the reason. Since most of the burners were very much naked, they wanted to conceal their real identity as much as possible.

My attention went to the guy who was seamlessly working at the bar of the camp, resembling Fry from Futurama. The only difference I found was that this Fry was conversing in Japanese fluently, causing my steps to maneuver closer to him on their own accord.

As I scanned a couple of bottles on the table, I asked, "What kind of sake do you have?"

"A few. Are you looking for a specific one?"

"I am not sure, but can I see them?" I was hoping to peek into the man's collection. As fate may have it, he presented before me three of his bottles that were kept in a cooler. Out of the three bottles, I found one to be Honjozo with an unfamiliar name of the brewery. Honjozo? I turned to face the man, "Where did you get this from?"

"A friend of mine got it from Tokushima, Japan."

You see, as per the U.S. Laws, any sake being sold here does not comply with the Japanese labeling laws. Honjozo Sake is not categorized as beer or wine rather it is categorized as a distilled spirit, whereas a Junmai sake is considered to be wine as per the Federal Alcohol Administration Act.

With the name "Honjozo" that is a premium sake, the distilled spirit added to it was to only enhance the level of alcohol, taste, and aroma of the sake, preserving the sake's unique taste. The distilled alcohol used was mixed to keep the alcohol percentage between the range of 15% and 17%. Still following the U.S. laws, if distilled alcohol is added throughout any production stage, it means the beverage is to be taxed 7 times higher.

Junmai has no additives, but Honjozo does, which is the distilled alcohol, leaving it to be priced higher with the higher tax, than a Junmai sake in the States. You see, before you purchase sake from Japan, you need to check the drink for its grade. The grading of sake is either Premium or Non-Premium. This was one thing I knew I had to delve into, as it goes on to show the preferences of sake drinkers.

Before we jump into knowing the different types of sake available, let's talk about the grade. Well, every time you buy sake from Japan, be mindful of checking the bottle for the grade labeled on the drink. While this does not hint that a non-premium sake is of low quality, it refers to the content of distilled alcohol used or not and is done so to cater to every type of taste bud.

The labeling on the bottles in Japan is as follows:

Premium: Tokutei Meisho-Shu, translates into specially named or designation sake.

Non-Premium: Futsu-Shu, translates into ordinary sake or table sake.

If you are a new to sake wanting to explore, my suggestion is to go for the premium as a safer bet. Now to further classify the premium sake, there are three more variations to it, namely Junmai, Ginjo, Daiginjo, and Honzojo. So if you are to come across a bottle of sake on which none of these words is present, then it is a clear indication that the bottle is a non-premium sake, known as Futsushu. Let's talk a little about the criteria for a sake to be categorized as *Premium*.

The very first is the Junmai and Honzojo. The other way to classify a sake as Premium is its duration of being fermented. If a sake is fermented for an extended period of time at low temperature using 60% polished rice with Ginjo yeast, it is classified as Ginjo and 50% or less is classified as Daiginjo. If such sake is free of additives such as distilled alcohol, then it is categorized as Junmai Ginjo and Junmai Daiginjo. If distilled alcohol is added, the bottles are called

Ginjo and Daiginjo.

'Seimai Buai'

Seimai Buai refers to the rice polishing ratio used in the brewing of sake. Even Ginjo has a sub-category known as Daiginjo, which translates to 'Super-Premium Ginjo.' The criteria are hard to meet for a sake to be classified as a Premium Ginjo. The process in itself is a criterion for the sake to be distinguished as either Tokubetsu (or special in English) Junmai or Tokubetsu Honjozo. As we understand that Seimai Buai refers to the percentage of polished rice ratio, to further break it down for your comprehension, Seimai Buai is used as an assessment tool that marks the percentage of rice grain remaining after the polishing process in terms of its weight. The lower the percentage of Seimai Buai, the more polished the rice is. If a sake that has a low Seimai Buai level, meaning the rice used is highly polished, it is more expensive as compared to one with a higher percentage of Seimai Buai.

This is because if most of the bran is scrubbed off from rice, it prevents the sake from being infiltrated with a high percentage of carbohydrates and minerals. Instead, a purer taste of the rice is retained, giving the sake a richer and refined taste. Hence, a Daiginjo is for the most expensive sake. Nonetheless, a Daiginjo might have a refined taste, letting the fans deem the entire process of Ginjo and Daiginjo to be at the peak of sake making.

In addition to these criteria, the inclusion of distilled alcohol in sake enhanced the taste and aroma of the sake, as well as adjusting it to the liking of the drinkers. When added in moderation during the brewing process, the alcohol aids in improving the aroma of the sake, while diluting its strong flavors. Due to this very reason, distilled alcohol is also incorporated in the making of Ginjo and Honjozo. Over the years, the patrons who are avid sake drinkers have reverted to the traditional taste of sake. Meaning, there has been a change in the pattern of sake preferences as people are opting more and more for the Junmai groups, inclusive of the Junmai-Shu and Junmai Ginjo-Shu.

Now that we have established the basics of what classifies a sake as Premium or Non-Premium, let's take a dive into the types of sake out there.

Junmai

So far, we have discussed Junmai enough for you to be able to tell the basic ingredients used to brew it. However, if you fail to recall, fret not. A Junmai is made from rice, water, koji, and yeast, with no distilled alcohol. Furthermore, as we speak of it, its classification is determined on the basis of the rice grain polished to about 70%. Due to the higher percentage of the rice kernel being polished, this enables the Junmai sake to have a far richer and stronger taste that contributes to its acidic nature, also called Umani. Hence, the reason a Junmai sake is most commonly served at room temperature or warm.

Honjozo

Honjozo is much like Junmai, the rice kernel is polished to about 70% before being used for the brewing. So what differentiates a Honjozo from Junmai? Above, we talked about how Junmai has a more distinct and acidic taste.

Thus, to even that out, a small percentage of distilled alcohol is added to the brew, which gives the concoction its title of being a Honjozo. Due to the addition of the distilled alcohol, the sake's aroma and flavors are balanced out to give even the new drinkers a fair-minded experience before they can develop a taste for Junmai. With the taste being lighter than Junmai, Honjozo sake is best served warm or chilled.

Ginjo and Junmai Ginjo

Junmai Ginjo is the simplest form of Ginjo sake and is the pure rice version. Ginjo is with additives such as distilled alcohol. The rice kernels needed to be polished off to an exact 60% and less.

Daiginjo and Junmai Daiginjo

Dai translates into big or super, hence a Daiginjo is specified as Super-Premium sake. As per the sake drinkers, a Daiginjo is the highest one can reach in the mastery and artistry of brewing sake. It is not every brewer's cup of tea as it requires precise measures to be maintained at all times.

Even the rice kernels used need to be polished to an exact 50% as the minimum benchmark. It is best served chilled (50°F) that does justice to its moderate yet sophisticated flavor and smell. A Junmai Daiginjo is a form of Daiginjo sake that falls under the same pure rice category. The only difference is that there is no addition of additives to it.

Futsushu

A Futsushu, or commonly known as Table Sake, is brewed from rice kernels that are only polished to 70-93%. This means the sake has a rather ordinary taste due to the lack of refined rice used and is not recommended to people who are new to the sake world. Now I am no Sommelier, but I would recommend any new person to stay away from Futsushu unless you want to end up nursing a bad hangover the next day. Due to the percentage of rice polished, this attributes to a Futsushu being less costly, but then again, you can still get a moderate sake for a lower price.

Shiboritate

As we have learned that sake is aged for a prolonged period of time like wine, it is certainly let to sit for fermentation for a minimum of six months. If a more mature taste is required, then the sake is left for more than half a year. A Shiboritate sake offers a 'like it or hate it' kind of a brew due to being bottled right after its pressing process. A Shiboritate sake is bottled and dispatched to the market straight off, skipping the maturing process altogether. Due to this, a Shiboritate has more of a fruity and rough taste, making some of its admirers associate it with white wine.

Nama-Zake

Usually, sake is pastulaized twice. First, after being brewed and the second right before being dispatched to markets. Nama-Zake, on the other hand, is unlike most sakes. It is unpastulized by heat not even once. Hence, for it to be preserved, the sake needs to be refrigerated at all times, until when the time of consumption comes. A bottle of Nama-Zake you can buy off the shelf is usually micro-filtered to weed out the germs rather than being sterilized by heat.

Namachozo

Unlike Nama-Zake, Namachozo sake is pastulized only once and that too during its final stage of production. As a result, it needs to be refrigerated at all times due to its opaque nature that also contributes to its refreshing, rich, and crisp taste.

Nigori

A Nigori (cloudy in English) sake is opaque in nature because it is coarsely meshed. This gives the liquid texture with rice particles floating in it. While the Nigori sake tends to be sweeter and creamier due to its opaque nature, the texture can vary from being silken smooth to coarse and concentrated. You might find it surprising that Nigori sake is served more in Japanese restaurants abroad than in Japan.

Jizake

Jizake translates into sake from a local artisanal producer. Jizake varies from region to region and is often brewed by smaller breweries. The taste is native to the area. So if you ever plan to travel throughout Japan, I would recommend you try Jizake. It is commonly served at restaurants with local cuisine, giving you a somewhat local taste of the region that will be unique to the place.

Infused Sake

An infused sake is gaining popularity rather rapidly amidst the drinkers due to the fruity flavors being added. A infused sake is preferred when mixing sake cocktails due to their intriguing taste and level of sweetness.

Akai Sake

Akai sake literally means red sake is fascinating. Unlike other sakes, it is reddish in color due to the use of a certain koji fungus used in the process. Definitely, the taste of Akai sake is as distinct as its color.

Taru Sake

I have shared how a sake can be manipulated by even the procedure and processes used. Well, Taru sake proves this. A sake, if stored in a cedar barrel, is referred to as Taru sake or a Cedar Shake in English. What makes a Taru sake unique is that the liquid adopts the woody taste from the cedar barrels, giving the sake a more earthy flavor and aroma, which many find to be rather comforting.

Sparkling Sake

As you must have guessed from the name, sparkling sake is bubbly in nature. When fermenting, it is brewed to a secondary level to lighten the alcohol. This gives it the sparkling characteristic along with a sweeter taste. It sets itself apart due to its lesser volume of alcohol in comparison with other sakes.

Kinpaku Sake

While a Kinpaku Sake has a similar taste to other forms of sake, the only reason this is pricier and different is the addition of gold flakes. It's served for holidays, birthdays, promotions, and engagement parties.

Arabashiri

A sake that is not allowed time to mature and bottled right after the meshing process is referred to as Arabashiri. Due to being meshed, the Arabashiri sake is distinct from its bulky nature, giving the drinkers a rather pleasant flavor.

Genshu

A Genshu sake is undiluted, giving you a thicker and richer taste as no water is added to dilute it before bottling. The undiluted sake washes the palate with a rich, ripe and fruit taste. Try on the rocks for a experience. It has a higher alcohol content that ranges from 16% to 20%.

Koshu

Koshu sake is left to be matured by the brewers for up to five years or more, allowing the taste to enhance, yet at the same time subdue itself evenly. Being left to age lets the sake absorb the barrel's earthiness, giving it an earthiness to itself, as well as an intense flavor.

Yamahai / Kimoto

With time as the brewing process of sake, there are still two types of sake made traditionally. Yamahai and Kimoto sake are quite alike, as they are brewed in a more labor-extensive manner. During the brewing process, a yeast starter is made traditionally that attributes to the sakes wilder and gamier taste. No lactic acids are added, but wild lactic bacteria are dripped into the open barrel where the Kurabito is kicking the mountain of rice off with the wooden oars, which is what leaves the sake to develop over a longer time frame. So what sets apart a Yamahai and Kimoto sake? Well, it is how the two liquids are left to obtain lactic acid produced by lactic bacteria from the environment during the production.

Classification of sake

Before the 1990s, the Japanese government used to label sake as Tokkyu (Special Class), Ikkyu (First Class), and Nikkyu (Second Class).

These labels had made it easy for the sake fanatics to locate their favorite brew as per their taste and budget. Over time, the way sake was categorized evolved. With time as the brewing process and recipes of a sake changed, a wider selection is available on the shelves of the market. This is why most new explorers, who want to try out the hype of sake for themselves, end up confused. By choosing the wrong type of sake that they might not like, some people have critiqued sake even before giving it a chance. Thus came the need to label sake with far more intricate details to give the buyer a quick overview of what to expect from the bottle before them. This greatly helps as the buyer is able to understand what the taste will be like and can pick a bottle as per their liking.

Chapter 3
Method of Sake Brewing

Is it easy to brew sake?

Before moving to New York, I used to live in Osaka and had come to know some people who grew up in Nada reigion of Hyogo prefecture. Nada is where famed sake breweries are majorly located. The people I came to know shared how they used to practice baseball on one of their teammate's few centuries-old sake brewery's grounds. They even shared how they saw ghosts flying through them while in elementary school for a few times.

I'm not too sure if their ghost story was true, but then it implies that there was some fatality associated with sake making. After all, the brewers needed to work as early as 2 am on a super cold winter morning, and they were there to watch how the fermentation was progressing all-day long for seven days a week.

Talking about Osaka, at the Burning Man BRC event, there was a theme camp next to us with a group of burners from Osaka that is led by Ken Hamazaki an Osaka native, also known as the "Red Tea Ceremony Contemporary Artist". He is famous in the Japanese burner community for conducting a traditional tea ceremony by the temple structure every year. Of course, no one was drinking sake in their camp, but some of them came to my sake bar and reluctantly tried some of my sake cocktails since they saw a crowd of topless young girls.

Traditional and Modern Methods

The process of brewing sake is rooted back to the 7th century when Koji was introduced in Nara. Around the 17th century, the Kimoto method was established. Even today, the process remains somewhat the same, but the Sake making is not so labor-intensive for the modern (Sokujo) method.

I had asked some of the burners from Osaka, as well as other patrons this: "Do you guys know that sake brewing dates back as late as the 7th century when Koji was first introduced in Nara?" Most of them did not care about history. I've seen some African American people come to the sake tasting room without knowing anything about Japan. It is very inspiring that the possibility of sake could become more widely distributed.

While sake brewing remains somewhat similar since Kimoto method was developed, but the modern (Sokujo) method is not as labor-intensive. Breweries had resorted to modern and semi-automated processes to ensure a smooth running of the entire production.

Is process of wine the same as sake? The answer is no. Wine is made from fermented sugar present in the fruits.

There is no need to use malt to convert the starch present in these fruits to sugar. The process of sake, on the other hand, is quite similar to that of making beer. Starch is first left to malting, then mashing, followed by boiling, and then fermenting that contributes to its intense taste.

Then why isn't sake just known as Japanese beer? Here is how the process of making sake differs from that of beer. Making sake is labor-intensive and extensive, and is a more complicated process. It involves some essential elements – rice, water, koji, yeast, and lactic acid for the modern method. The seasoned-skilled brewers can adjust the process based on temperatures and other elements. Water and rice are vital to the brewing process and take up to as much as 80% of the content.

Before I dive into the detailed step-by-step process of sake brewing, allow me to make one thing clear. I mentioned above how skills are an essential element in the brewing process. Generally speaking, only an expert can brew sake, an expert who is skilled and well versed with the right amount of ingredients to be added, especially the yeast. This is true when employing the Kimoto method but, modern sake brewing can be produced by using data. Either way, the expert must also have a brewery in a temperature-controlled area to ensure the sake does not rot during its maturing process.

Next, let's move on to find out the process that takes place in making sake.

Steps

The details of the sake making process are not very well known, and how to make sake is a bit complicated for most of us. Generally, there are in total about 12 steps involved in making sake.

Step 1: Rice Milling/Polishing

The very first step is Rice Milling. Once the desired sake rice reaches the brewery, the milling process initiates. There are many varieties of rice that brewers choose for sake. They are called Saka Mai or Shuzo Kotekimai translating to Sake Rice. The most common of them used are Yamadanishiki, Gohyakumangoku, Miyamanishiki, and Omachi. The reason why these types of rice are preferred is due to the nature of the grain. The grains are bigger and sturdier than table rice, which makes them less prone to breakage during Rice Milling. The type of sake the brewer wishes to produce determines what type of rice they want to use.

The rice grains are milled to remove their bran and layers to access the starch pockets. Only Saka Mai has the core of the rice, known as Shinpaku, which has an opaque white core.

The amount of rice polished off depends on the variant of sake being brewed. The minimum percentage polished off is higher than the type of rice consumed for eating. The reason being, the outer layers contain other nutrients and minerals, such as fats and protein, which can result in a patchy taste of the drink. The part most essential to sake brewing is the starch in the rice grain, so the rice kernels are polished to up to 70%. This process can take up to 48-72 hours. If the brewers are to use a less-milled rice grain to make sake, it will result in the starch not fully seeping within the concoction. Hence more rice grain will be required. Thus, brewers prefer to polish the rice kernels as much as possible to reduce the quantity of rice to be used. Currently, the milling machine is used to control the rice polishing ratio. A sake bottle label states the rice polishing ratio to be 60%, it means that 40% of the rice grain was milled.

Step 2: Washing and Soaking

The next step is washing and soaking the milled rice in the brewing process. The milled rice cannot be directly used to produce sake as there is a residue left behind. To ensure that the rice grain is free of the powdered residue, the rice grains are carefully washed. This step requires precision and delicacy. That's because if the rice grains are washed harshly, they will break, and the result will be poor.

Once the rice grains are washed and free from Nuka (residue), the washed rice is put to be soaked. The brewers need to control the time duration of the soaking process as it significantly affects the result too. If the rice grains aren't soaked for long enough, once again, it will affect the amount of starch seeping into the concoction and will result in a lighter taste. If the rice is soaked for too long, it will result in the grains turning mushy, and will produce a different variation of sake.

The duration for soaking rice depends on the end product brewers are trying to produce. This step also affects the next stage of steaming rice because the longer the rice grain is soaked for, the more moisture it absorbs. The brewers do not want a rice grain that is either too rigid or too soggy. They want the grain to still be intact until the last few steps.

Step 3: Steaming

Once the rice has been prepared, the brewing process starts. The soaked rice is collected and then placed in industrial steamers. In this process, the brewer needs to maintain precaution and steam the rice in accordance with the desired result. Unlike how we steam rice when cooking, here the rice is kept separate from the water. Yes, the rice isn't placed in water and then steamed. Instead, rice is placed over a thin net, and the brewers allow steam to reach the rice from the bottom. This process is known as Koshiki.

Typically, brewers steam rice for about an hour. It allows for the rice grain to absorb moisture, while the heat goes on to change the molecular structure of the rice kernel. It starts to break down the starch within the core of the rice grain, leading to a softer inner core while the outer layer of the rice remains firm in its texture. Some brewers cater to a diverse range of sake separate the steam rice for their next step. While some of the steamed rice is kept for the Koji molt cultivation, some are sent directly for the fermentation process.

Brewers maintain precaution and do not leave the rice to rest after being steamed, as by doing so, it would allow for the rice to cool down. If the rice is left to cool, it would mean the heat will get more time to penetrate within the rice grain and affect their texture. Thus, as soon as the rice is steamed, brewers send the rice to the next step.

Step 4: Koji Making

The Koji making process is what sake brewers often call the 'Heart' of the entire sake making. Rice-based Koji is the rice used in making sake that will have the mold growing on it. Koji is the mold that covers these prepared rice grains.

After the rice is steamed, it is moved to a room with a

higher concentration of humidity. The walls of this room are either of wood or metal to trap heat in them. This contributes to the right temperature needed for the molds to grow on the rice grain. The rice is spread out on a large table, where it is allowed to cool from the outside, while the inside is left to remain hot. By doing so, the brewers allow the mold the right balance of humid temperature to feed on the moisture within the rice kernel. This way, the entire rice kernel gets treated by the koji.

The brewers continuously check on the rice grains to know when they are cooled to the optimum temperature. If they leave the rice to cool thoroughly, then the koji process wouldn't be able to take place. Cooling down the rice is important, too. If the rice doesn't achieve the right temperature, the mold won't cover the entire rice grain and will only feed on the outer layer of the rice grain. After the rice cools down, the koji spores, which are yellowish and fine, are sprinkled all over the rice grain. The koji-covered steamed rice is then separated into smaller trays and moved to a darker room with controlled temperature, then is left to rest for 2-4 days. The brewer then continues to check on the rice each day to ensure the koji making is taking place. The mold is supposed to cover the rice and change its texture entirely.

In the darkroom, the rice is tossed and continuously

mixed to ensure the rice based koji-making (kome-koji) process takes place. During this time, the brewer continues to sprinkle koji at least four more times, depending on the amount needed. The koji that the brewer sprinkles are made fresh every time when they spray it over the rice. By the end of the process, a rice kernel is supposed to have a frosted appearance and a sweet but subtle aroma of chestnuts.

The usage of fresh koji each time ensures the mold is active enough to do the work and trickle to the core of the rice grain. Once this step is covered, the treated rice grains are then moved for the next stage.

Step 5: Shubo/Moto (Fermentation)

Once the rice-based koji is ready, the extensive process of fermentation begins, known as either: Shubo, for the modern method, or Moto, a puree of rice or base of fermentation for the Kimoto method. Shubo refers to the yeast starter and is what aids the conversion of glucose to alcohol. To begin, Shubo is concocted from steamed rice, water, koji-rice, and yeast. Both the steamed rice and koji are obtained from the steps above.

After all of the ingredients are added to a barrel. It left to activate the yeast in it for at least two weeks. For the Kimoto and Yamahai method, a wild lactic acid produced in the process takes care of any germs present in the concoction and kills them for the modern method the brewers add it. By the end of the two weeks, the Shubo has a denser and a concentrated percentage of yeast.

Step 6: Moromi (Main-Mash)

In this step, more rice-based koji, water, and steamed rice are added to the Shubo. This addition forms a new concoction known as Moromi. The contribution of yeast to the Shubo aids in the fermentation of Moromi. Moromi is left to ferment for 24-36 hours so that the yeast begins its dividing process. The second step, known as Nakazoe, begins on the 3rd day of Moromi being prepared. This process is the repetition of the first one, where more rice-based koji, steamed rice, and water are added. Then the mixture is left to sit for another 24 hours before the final step takes place.

The third step, known as Tomezoe, is the same as the steps above. It involves the final addition of koji, steamed rice, and water to the Moromi. Over 4-5 days, koji, steamed rice, and water are added gradually, allowing for a proper fermentation of yeast in each batch to take place. This ensures a smoother end product at the very end.

Such a fermentation allows for the starch to break down into glucose and then convert into alcohol easily. The batch is incorporated in smaller quantities so that it consumes less time to brew. Here comes an interesting aspect that separates sake from any other form of liquor. While other alcohol, and even beer, are fermented in separate barrels, sake is fermented in the same barrel since the beginning of its process.

In one barrel, the slow addition of Shubo to Moromi causes both processes to take place together. The koji is what breaks down the starch in the rice to glucose and the yeast added turns that glucose into alcohol. The Moromi is then left to ferment for a period of 18 days to a month.

With a raw sake produced at this stage, the Moromi is then passed to other steps of sake making.

Step 7: Pressing/Joso

With the Moromi fermentation and producing a rawer version of sake, the liquid is then passed on to the Pressing process, also known as Joso. During Joso, the liquid is separated from the clear liquid and the unfermented solid remains of rice grains. In the modern times, this pressing is done by automated machines called Yabuta, but in the olden times, the Moromi would be placed in bags and then hanged to let the clear sake drip into a container. Today, breweries that continue to practice the old methods employ the same technique.

In a Yabuta, there are multiple metal frames stacked in

the machine, on top of which the Moromi is poured. The sides of the Yabuta are then 'squeezed', exerting pressure on the liquid to pass through the meshed-line frames. This way, the solid particles stay behind, known as Sake Kasu, or sake grounds in English, and the liquid sake is collected. At the end of the process, as the machine is opened, and the meshed-frames are removed, the Kasu can be peeled off of them.

Step 8: Filtration

After Joso, the collected liquid undergoes filtration to ensure that the sake is pure, and no residue is left. There are some options for the filtration and often charcoal powder is used as a preferred filter. Given the porous nature of the charcoal, it makes it a great filter as it holds back dead yeast, enzymes, and other tiny molecules within the liquid, inclusive of remaining starch. Once the charcoal powder is churned into the sake mix, it is then passed through another chamber that is lined with a special filter paper that holds back the charcoal and allows for a clearer and brighter liquid to pass through sake. The production of sake does not end here, there are still a few more steps before the sake reaches the market.

Step 9: Pasteurization

After filtration, some brewers sell the sake right away, which is known as Nama-Zake, which literally means 'raw sake' or 'unpasteurized sake' and the bottles are refrigerated at all times to prevent the sake from rotting.

There are two ways to pasteurize a sake. The first method is done by passing sake through a pipe, which is until the temperature of the sake reaches 150°F. The machine is then used as a simple pasteurization machine, resulting in the sake to last on its own. The second method involves placing sake in either bottles or pipes, then they are submerged in hot water until the temperature of the sake reaches 150 °F. In both methods, allowing the temperature of the sake to reach 150°F. After pasteurization, the sake is ready to either be aged or bottled, as per the brewer's preference.

Step 10: Aging

After pasteurization, the taste of sake is sturdy and distorted to an extent. Thus, brewers often leave the sake in a tank (or barrel) so that the flavor of the sake can even out. Each tank is left in storage for a minimum of 3 to 6 months, depending on the variation of sake being produced. Once the sake is out a tank, it is ready for the last step that is bottling.

Step 11: Bottling

Sake that is pasteurized and aged undergo pasteurization once again. After taking the sake out of storage, the alcohol content is still high at 22%. This means that the sake needs to be diluted with water to lower the percentage of alcohol to about 15%. After the alcohol level is lowered to eliminate any pollutants that could have entered the sake or any last bit of active enzymes or yeast within the brew, the clear liquid is pasteurized once again before bottling.

Step 12: Storage

After the bottles are ready to be shipped to the markets, some even to be exported, we reach the crucial point of safely storing the bottles. While we know sake, like Nama-zake, needs to be refrigerated at all times, it is advisable to refrigerate both the Nama-Chozo and the Nama-Zume sake once the bottles are opened for consumption.

It is advised to keep the bottles in the dark place rather than having them being exposed to sunlight. The most bottles of sake are either frosted, ambered or even green in nature. The color of the bottle helps reflect the UV rays from making contact with the sake. Furthermore, the best temperature to store sake is below 59 °F.

Once you bring a bottle of sake home, continue to care for it by properly storing it. Keep the lid secured at all times to prevent the sake from being exposed to air. Keep the bottle either refrigerated or at room temperature to prevent the taste from changing. If you maintain and properly store your bottle, you can prevent the sake from oxidizing and furthermore, preserve its taste for a longer period of time.

Storing sake the way it deserves concludes the lengthy and extensive brewing process of sake. Now we can understand better why sake is highly raved about all over the world, apart from being Japan's preferred liquor. The quality of the ingredients are premium, the steps are precise, and the skillful art involved in the making of sake is mesmerizing.

After this chapter, I am sure that the next time you see a bottle of sake, you will know about the bottle's long journey it had to have endured before hitting the shelves.

Chapter 4
Rice, Water, Koji, and Yeast

Can sake be an alternative to water?

In BRC, on the third day, Eizo, all of a sudden, started serving a shot of Vodka with his octopus sushi by saying, "Drink a shot of Vodka with my sushi to kill some germs in your stomach."

Again, no patrons understood the Japanese language at the bar except for me. So I asked, "Doesn't sushi usually use wasabi instead of Vodka?" He replied, "No, wasabi alone won't..." the good thing was that no one enjoying his sushi understood Japanese. After all, we were on Playa, and the temperature was high and so even this high-end Vodka wasn't too enticing.

Unlike wine in Europe, sake isn't consumed alternatively to water. I went to Paris about a few decades ago from Osaka. A guide of a small group of Japanese mentioned a story of how French people used to drink wine in the morning as drinkable water, which was far more expensive in most of Europe. Also, the French schoolchildren were used to drinking wine between lessons. As odd as it may seem, the reason behind it was under the impression that alcohol killed microbes, and it at least seemed to help with warming the chest when a child was suffering from a cold.

You see, the cost of brewing Junmai sake is expensive

and is heavily taxed, or at least used to be. For a long time, sake was served only to people who could afford it, until the government allowed sake brewers to add distilled alcohol, and sweetener to reduce the time to market while lowering the production cost.

A production cost is high but priced low

Currently, there seems to be an ongoing trend and an ever-growing fandom for Sake around the globe, yet many visitors traveling to Tokyo remain oblivious to the pricing strategy of sake. While high-end restaurant-goers are accustomed to paying a hefty cost for the sublime drink, they are astounded to know how cheaply-priced sake can be in Japan.

The pricing of sake does not reflect the fact that exported sake is doing well. For example, a bottle of imported Junmai Daiginjo is sold for $50 in Berkeley, while it's less than half of that price in Japan. The export of the sake is projected to be tripled in 2020 to over $600M from the $200M in 2018. I once asked the head of the sales department of a brewery in Berkeley,

"Why don't we price our sake a bit more like a bottle of wine?"

He said,

"…the pricing of sake is not that simple There are way

too many competitors producing almost the same variety and that forces us to stay competitive with the low price."

This trend is something too commonly seen at the Japanese grocery store in San Francisco. Every year, the sake section expands with domestic and imported bottles. When I look at a 750ml flavored sake bottle from the same brewery, for instance, their competitors produce a similar sake at $1 cheaper.

In comparison, if sake was priced like wine, the sales would be at least $100B. This is an instant giveaway to how low the price for Sake was. I believe that sake brands that offer an exquisite taste should be priced at a higher value. There is a 720 ml bottle of Junmai Ginjo sake that is made from at least 60% polished rice with the finest water, Koji, and yeast, yet no added alcohol offers a denser aroma. Such sake is still priced at $15 in Tokyo. Now, this price falls within the same range as a table wine, leaving many overseas-based consumers confused as to how a premium beverage costs the same as table wine. In comparison, French wine of a similar quality is priced at least $400-$500 across liquor stores in Japan itself.

This led the Foreign Ministry in Japan to conclude that while France made an effort to launch an awareness campaign to their wine, marketing costs were passed on to consumers at a higher price compared to sake, and therefore was not able to compete with Japanese brands who did not do the same. It is known that Japanese sake is made by Toji (the master brewer), and Kurabito (the sake brewers), who pour their heart and soul into the brewing process, yet the price falls slightly above the profit line with creating a deeper desire within Japanese consumers to buy their products as opposed to wine.

A Cost of Raw Materials

As intricate as the brewing process is, the same amount of care is given to the chosen ingredients to brew the sake. Each ingredient has a vital role in the production of sake. The ingredients used are rice, koji, water and yeast.

Rice

The very first ingredient is rice, which is what sake is renowned for. Who could have thought that liquor could be brewed from rice when it's a staple diet, right? But such has been the tale in Japan for as old as time.

Sake, however, is not produced from just any type of rice grain. First, you need to understand that sake rice is very different from the kind of rice we consume, which is known as 'Food Rice'.

Sakamai is larger grain than food rice

Sakamai is known as the brewer's rice, otherwise known as

sake-rice. The very first difference between sake rice has larger kernels compared to food rice.

Shinpaku

Regular food rice grains have no prominent core while sake rice grains have an opaque core that is integral to brewing sake. This is commonly known as the starch pocket, or Shinpaku in Japanese. This core is what makes the rice unique and gives sake its texture and taste. The outer layer of rice that is polished off is what comprises protein and fats in which the brewers called them as miscellaneous elements.

Brewing Sustainability of Sake Rice

The starch, however, has a semi-fluid consistency. It is easy to melt this starch once the koji infests the polished rice grain, thus making the rice a good absorbent as it soaks up the rest of the flavors during the brewing process. Even when steamed, the rice does not lose its form but absorbs the water to melt the Shinpaku, which gives the koji molt the optimum environment to cultivate.

While these prominent differences make sake rice desirable to be used in making sake, there are still over 80 types of rice grown to make sake in Japan. Among the many kinds of sake rice, four types of sake rice are desired the most by brewers. Each type has its own unique property, making different types of sake rice desirable when making different types of sake.

These four types of sake rice are Yamadanishiki, Omachi, Gohyakumangoku, and Miyamanishiki. Yamadanishiki and Omachi sake rice are referred to as the *Okute type*. Whereas, Gohyakumangoku and Miyamanishiki are variations of sake rice known as *Wase type*. The ***okute type*** of sake rice is harder to harvest and can only be grown in colder regions.

Okute

An Okute type of sake rice is the type that offers a more ripe and succulent taste with a decadent texture.

Yamadanishiki

Yamadanishiki sake rice originates and is mainly harvested in Hyogo prefecture. Some of the rice farmers in Fukuoka and Tokushima are harvesting it nowadays with the high pricing of its nature. Yamadanishiki sake rice is considered regal because it has retained its properties since the year 1912, coupled with its long history gives Yamadanishiki the title of being the 'King of Rice'. Yamadanishiki is the most preferred sake rice by brewers as it is palatable and has a decadent taste. This rice costs 2x more than regular table rice sold in Japan.

Omachi

Omachi sake rice originated from the Okayama district after the Edo period. Now it is commonly grown in Okayama, Hiroshima, and Gifu. Given the texture of an Omachi rice grain, sake brewed from these kernels have a stronger taste. I do not recommend newbies to try sake brewed from Omachi due to the hard taste of the drink. The reason for an Omachi Rice grain having a complex taste is due to the fact it requires a more specialized environment and cultivated soil. Even today, not everyone can plow and sow Omachi rice.

Wase

Wase type of sake rice was cultivated after WWII due to the shortage of rice. Wase gave farmers a higher yield of rice, at the same time to grow different kinds of rice as opposed to the Okute type. As a result, the Wase type of sake rice was cultivated. The Wase type has a riper and crisper taste because the rice grains are cleaner and harder to dissolve in Moromi. Due to this, the starch is converted to alcohol without the grain losing its texture. This contributes toward a clearer sake liquid.

Gohyakumangoku

Gohyakumangoku rice originates from the Niigata prefecture and is commonly grown in not just Niigata, but also in other regions such as Fukui and Toyama. The grains are larger, making it easier for brewers to polish them without the grain crumbling. The starch pocket, too, is larger, attributing towards a clearer and crisp Sake that is refreshing in taste.

Miyamanishiki

Miyamanishiki is a special type of Wase sake rice. It was initially grown as a variant to Takashinishiki in 1978, a sudden mutation happened when the Miyamanishiki was exposed to another variety of rice, Takane Nishiki, that was then exposed to gamma radiation. The thing that stood out was its shinpaku: a "whiter than white" white-heart to rival the snow-capped peaks of a mountain range that was named as such: Miyama. Miyama literally translates to "the beautiful peaks." This variant can be sourced from Nagano, Akita, Yamagata, Iwate, and many other districts. Since it is carefully cultivated in the northern parts of Japan, the Miyamanishiki rice kernel produces a more refined, clean, and silky sake.

Sake production is no easy job, and we are just getting started on how carefully each ingredient and step is monitored. Knowing the types of rice and the careful selection of them, let's look into the next ingredient and how it plays a role in offering sake many different textures.

Koji

Koji is the essential mold in brewing sake. Koji breaks down the starch within the rice kernel and converts it into glucose which is later fermented into alcohol.

Koji-malt or Koji-kin is a harmless fungus that is cultivated beforehand to be sprinkled onto the steamed sake rice during the brewing process. The rice is then left in a dark room for the koji to gnaw and penetrate it to reach the starch within to break their molecular structure. There are multiple varieties of Koji and the type of koji used for brewing is the yellow Koji.

Koji begins by breaking the starch apart within the rice to turn it into glucose so that it is prepared for its next process where Shubo, the yeast, is added to it. With the enzymes that Koji released, the process at which is known as saccharification, allows the yeast to easily convert the glucose into alcohol and release the trapped carbon dioxide from within the concoction.

As the sake rice is polished, the husk on the outer layers is scrubbed off. This means all the enzymes present within the rice grain are removed, hence requiring an additional catalyst to assist the process of alcohol making.

This is where these distinctive yellow koji spores come in, they are generously sprinkled over the steamed rice, releasing their enzymes and beginning the process. Note that while the primary purpose of this koji-kin mold is to break down the starch into glucose, it is also to give the sake a sweeter taste.

So, how is koji made? The process of making koji is known as Seigiku, which begins in a temperature-controlled room within the brewery that is solely used for breeding koji mold. The room is labeled as Koji-Muro (koji room) by the brewers. You'll be surprised to know that koji is extracted from steam rice. Hence, when ready, koji is mixed with more rice later on.

This is where yeast is added too and begins the process of the yeast converting the glucose, along with koji, constantly breaking down starch. The process of koji making can easily take up to 3-5 days. The brewers within this time frame regularly check on the rice, which is placed in a temperature and light-controlled room. These factors play a vital role in the koji to form and start the process of saccharification. If the temperature is too harsh or if the rice grains are exposed to light, koji mold can destroy themselves instead of breaking the starch content.

Brewers know that the koji is ready when the rice appears frosted. This means the koji has infested the rice grain. Apart from the frosted appearance, koji gives off a chestnut fragrance along with a sweeter taste. Workers can taste the rice as koji is a harmless mold.

With time as the entire process of sake became

modernized, so did the process of koji making. The use of automated machinery is to speed up the process of sake making to meet with the consumption demands of the market. As a result, where previously koji would require a couple of days to be produced, now with this machinery, it can only take up to 42 hours.

Water

While rice is the soul to sake, water is the heart of it, as 80% of sake is water. Hence, a good water source is crucial in making the perfect sake. Ask a brewer the importance of water, and they might tell you it is as important as a key is to a locked door.

Water is added multiple times during the entire brewing process. This makes it very crucial for the brewers to ensure the quality of the water they use remains consistent to prevent any alteration of taste in the final product.

Water that is used for sake brewing is known as Shuzo-Yosui in Japanese or 'brewer's water' in English. There is, however, a conflict when it comes to the correct usage of water because most brewers prefer to wash, soak, and steam the rice as well. You will be surprised to know that during the brewing process, the amount of water used can weigh up to 110 lb more than the amount of rice used. Brewer's water, as mentioned above, is used throughout the process from washing and soaking the rice, to making the Moromi that ferments sake. When it comes to bottling the sake, the brewer's water is no longer used. Instead, Binzume-Yosui (bottling water) is used to wash the bottles that will be filled and to dilute the sake beforehand.

Having discussed the two classifications of water and their purpose in sake brewing, let's move towards the sources, the properties of the water used, and how they impact sake.

Sources of Water

Water used in sake brewing is usually either taken from local springs or rivers due to their high mineral content. The mineral content is vital in sake brewing if a brewer uses tap water for sake, they have to enrich the water with added minerals, in the hopes of enhancing the taste of the sake. The most famous spots for taking water used to be rivers and springs.

Fukuryusi, is the water flows through and down a moss-covering stone wall, and is obtained from Mt. Fuji in the Shizuoka prefecture.

Miyamizu, which is an abbreviation of "Nishinomiya no mizu" or Nishinomiya water is drawn from wells in the Nada region beneath Nishinomiya City. Gokosui is the natural spring water that is listed as one of the 100 most excellent natural water resources in Japan. It can be obtained from the Fushimi region of Kyoto district.

A challenge the brewers are facing everywhere is climate change. It became hard for them to rely on rivers, spring lakes and deep wells to source water for sake.

Another issue is the increased pollution. As a result, they had little to no choice to either chemically alter or filter the water, synthetically producing water, or enriching tap water with minerals instead.

Hard and Soft Water

There are two types of water: Kohsui (hard water) and Nansui (soft water). For example, Miyamizu is considered as hard water while Gokosui is considered as soft water. Hard water is the most sought after water type in the sake brewing process due to its high calcium and magnesium content, which leads to a richer sake taste. Soft water has a lower calcium and magnesium content and as a result, the end product is lighter and clearer sake.

Good Minerals

Water that has a high content of potassium, phosphoric acid, and magnesium is vital for sake. Without these minerals, the brewing process would be significantly affected. These minerals are vital to helping the yeast in the Shubo breed properly and boost the koji's infestation. Without these minerals, the yeast will fail to work at the right speed, hence altering the fermentation process altogether, which can result in a rotten concoction. Although these minerals are essential, it poses a problem for the brewers: Potassium is a water-soluble mineral and most of it is purged during the washing and soaking process of the rice. Brewers have to be very careful during these processes and have to be mindful of time because if they overdo any step, they will lose the potassium.

Another challenge the brewer needs to tackle is that phosphoric acid is attached to other fat and protein molecules. They have to carefully remove these molecules so that when they break the acid's chemical bonds, the enzymes would only propagate the yeast and aid in the further development of the koji instead of hurting it.

It is no easy task to manage these precautions. One minor mistake can lead to the entire brewing process to go awry. One trivial error and the whole taste of the sake can be ruined.

Yeast

Once koji does its work of breaking down the starch, brewers then move on to the next step, which is Shubo. Shubo is what comprises yeast in it, which then further breaks down the glucose into alcohol. Brewers need to add yeast in the right amount, as too little or too much will have adverse effects on the drink.

To ensure the end taste of the sake is delectable, and that the flavors and aroma do not overpower one another, yeast needs to be carefully added. To clear this picture a little more, let me ask you, what is one sense that attracts humans the most to food and beverages? It is the sense of smell. Now imagine if you are to drink a liquid that smells foul, will you gulp it down? No, right?

Sake experts have classified three types of fragrances that are produced when drinking sake. The first is the general whiff that we take when opening the bottle. This should be pleasant enough for the person to be intrigued by the drink.

The second whiff is known as Fukumi-Ka that a consumer will sense when they are drinking the sake. Again, if the smell or taste is too bitter or too dull, it will give off a negative sense and will not be pleasant for consumption.

The third type of smell that the drinker will sense is described as Midori-Ka that will be produced after the sake is ingested and will be present in the breath. Would you want to drink a liquid that gives you bad breath? Absolutely not. Yeast, however, affects all three stages of smell, hence making it vital to be carefully adding in the right amount.

Yeast needs to be present throughout the Moromi process

to convert the glucose into alcohol. A variety of yeast presents an opportunity to produce different sakes. Yeasts used in the sake brewing process are only officially distributed by the Japan Brewery Association to maintain quality. The types of yeast they distribute are known as Kyokai Kobo.

Brewers prefer a different variation of yeast that best suits their brewing methods and the type of sake they wish to produce. The wide variety of yeast is denoted a number and distributed by the Japanese Brewery Association.

Number One

Uncommon yeast strain and it was isolated in 1906 from shubo at Sakuramasamune in Nada.

Number Two

Uncommon yeast strains and it was isolated from shubo at Gekkeikan in Fushimi.

Number Three to Five

Uncommon yeast strains from Hiroshima.

Number Six

Number Six yeast is isolated at Aramasa in Akita and is one of the most popular yeast strains. It works the fastest as an enzyme, giving off a somewhat regulated fragrance. It gives the concoction an intricate taste and is best used when brewers want to produce a clear sake, such as the Kimoto-type sake.

Number Seven

Number Seven yeast offers a more refreshing and aromatic nature to the sake. The taste, however, is still intricate. Brewers use Number Seven yeast commonly for the production of Ginjo, Futsu-Shu, and Kimoto-type sake.

Number Nine

Number Nine yeast is also labeled as Kumamoto-Kobo as it's a relatively slower enzyme, working best at lower temperatures. Hence, if a brewery is within colder regions of Japan, brewers would go for Number Nine yeast, which offers an intense aroma. Number Nine yeast is mainly used to produce Ginjo Sake.

Number Fourteen

Much like Number Nine, Number Fourteen yeast is labeled as Kanagawa-Kobo. This offers the sake a stronger acidic taste while producing a fruitier smell that often deludes the drinkers to think the drink has melon or pear extract. Number Fourteen yeast is used by brewers when they want to make Ginjo and must be fermented slow and cold.

Number Fifteen

Number Fifteen yeast also offers an acidic taste with strong notes of a fruity and floral scent to sake. Hence, this is only used when brewers want to make a more enhanced variation of sake. This strain of yeast ferments at low temperatures.

Lactic Acid

During each step of sake brewing, enzymes, nutrients, and bacteria are grown. A handful of bacteria is unwanted, hence requiring a substance that would eliminate these harmful bacteria to ensure the quality of sake is sustainable with a longer shelf-life.

Lactic acid is a necessary addition in the Shubo to help remove bacteria and regulate the aroma and flavors of the concoction. Brewers prefer to add lactic acid to enhance the flavoring of the end product. It gives sake a slightly acidic taste to even out the sweetness of the beverage.

Now, lactic acid can be introduced to the mixture in two ways — either the **Kimoto-type** or the **Sokujo-type.**

Kimoto-type lactic acid

This type of lactic acid is already present within the brewery, and the brewers add it back to the mixture during the Shubo process.

Sokujo-type lactic acid

This is the most common form of lactic acid that brewers use. It is store-bought and in liquid form, making lactic acid work faster in killing the bacteria present within the mixture. Taking careful steps and monitoring each ingredient used ensures the credibility of sake in the market. This is why each bottle of sake we enjoy always tastes its best till the very last sip.

Chapter 5
History of Sake

Sake's roots in Nara and Kyoto

The history of sake is as rich as the various tastes available on the shelf in the market. You may be surprised to know the history of sake brewing can be dated back to 500 B.C.

Let's go back in time to see how sake was made that we enjoy today. To familiarize those who are new to the Japanese culture, I'll start with an episode at BRC. During the daytime, I needed to kill time alone at the Playa as my tent would start roasting. I would be cruising around the city on my rented bike while most of the camp members were comfortably sleeping in their pods, vans, and RVs until nighttime. During one of such cruising of mine, I stumbled upon a camp called Playa Choir. They were practicing gospel songs. I had stopped and parked my bike by the dome to watch them perform. Then an elderly lady who said she was 85 years old told me that I could be part of the choir. She gave me a piece of paper to fill out my contact information, after which she gave me a few musical scores.

I was born into a Buddhist family where everybody chanted "Nam-Myo-Ho-Renge-Kyo". My parents were very devout and stopped me from attending the annual summer parade hosted by a Shinto religious group. It was the same as telling a child to not participate in trick-or-treating during

Halloween because they weren't pagan.

This chanting sometimes appears in films and TV shows like Back to the Future, Tina Turner, and most recently, Lucious Lyon was chanting it in the TV show, Empire.

My fascination with gospel began after I had seen a choir in a church located on West 125th Street in Harlem, New York. I had gone there with a Japanese TV crew, a couple of comedians, and singers who had their very own talk show in Tokyo.

I was hired by a Japanese advertising agency to conduct a marketing design for their Harlem tour campaign. This was almost 3 decades ago, and around the time, 125th Street in Manhattan was not a tourist destination. On the contrary to Harlem's notorious reputation, there were a few tour buses filled by all-white Americans. These tourists came to the Apollo Theater to see the amateur standup comedy show that usually happened on Saturday nights. Then the tour continued to the Soul food restaurant, and then to the Gospel church.

Back at the Playa, I had joined the choir. The choir practiced from 10 am – 1 pm daily and I managed to kill two birds with one stone and joined as a soprano, no longer needing to cruise endlessly around the Playa.

Their premise was to perform last Sunday by the temple at sunrise, which was around 5 am. The temple burn is a finale of the event and usually happens Sunday night. All of the structures have different designs every year. The competitions select winners, and the artist who won can build the structure. The 2019 temple design was modeled after the Fushimi Inari Shinto Shrine, and I called this temple selection is an idiosyncrasy. It was titled "The Temple of Direction" by Geordie Van Der Bosch:

"The Temple of Direction happens to be a linear space, entailing the elegance and austerity of **the torii gates at Fushimi Inari Shrine in Japan**, where the artist had resided. The linear lines craft a transit, expanding into an enormous hallway, breathing both a physical experience and an emblematic journey. It's a grand opening of space that embraces the openness of the playa by creating a skeleton that hypes the participants to travel from one end to another.

This linear form is known to be depicting the journey of life with its beginning, middle, and end. Throughout the architecture, there are markings that mirror this journey: narrow & wide spaces, bright & dark spaces, and excavates that create a personal and bodily atmosphere. At the same time, an enormous chief hall, an altar, and countless shelves for offerings establish a medium for our shared encounter. Lanterns in the exterior and interior of the 180-foot-long, 37-foot-wide, 36-foot-high Temple. There were four entrances facing the four cardinal directions of the BRC -12,

3, 6, and 9 o'clock."

On the day we performed, surprisingly, the Choir distanced themselves about 200ft away from the temple. After one or two songs were sung, a priest came in front of the crowd and started preaching. He said,

"...before you came to a Burning Man, did you consult anybody about what to wear? "

There were about 200 spectators in front of us.

"You know they should've asked us if we like the temple like that…"

Evidentially, the choir group didn't like the Shinto Shrine temple. I mused to myself, ironically, the Christian priest and my Buddhist parents had something in common.

Coincidentally, the Original Fushimi Inari Shrine is located in Fushimi within the Southern part of Kyoto City in Kyoto prefecture. It also happens to be a historical place for sake and had the first sake brewery that had a sake tasting room. The Onigiri (rice ball) shop where I saw the 'Help Wanted' ad leading to the testing room was named Tamon, and owned by a former employee of the same brewery and is from the Fushimi area.

The history of sake including where and how sake came to still remains uncertain. The first recorded reference to the usage of alcohol in Japan was scribed in the book of Wei falling under the Records of the Three Kingdoms. The Book of Wei is a 3rd Century Chinese script that narrates the Japanese drinking and dancing. Within the book, Kojiki, a Japanese alcohol beverage is mentioned quite a few times.

In the Nara era of 710-794, Prince Shotoku, the founder of Nara that was once the capital city, built an imperial palace modeled after the Tang Dynasty court. He had invited Chinese laborers for design and construction. These Chinese laborers had introduced Koji. It is also known that right after the capitol was built, sake was reserved for religious ceremonies, court festivals, and other drinking games.

It was no surprise that sake gained popularity, and it became a government monopoly tool for years. Only by the 10th century did a temple named Tamon-In in Fushimi started to brew sake, hence birthing the main center of production for the next 500 years to come.

In a Tamon-In Diary, written by the monks of Tamon-In temple from 1478-1618, it entailed many details about the brewing process the temple used to follow. From pasteurization to the process of adding more ingredients during the main fermentation, that is they added starter mesh, steamed rice and water to the three stages they had developed, all was written in detail. By the 16th century, the distillation process adapted and practiced was introduced by the Ryukyu (Okinawa) in the Kyushu region. By then the brewing of Shochu was commonly practiced, known as Imo-Sake, and then was sold at the main market of Kyoto. Now let's take a look at each step in history in detail.

Earliest known production in 500 B.C.

While it is difficult to pinpoint the exact discovery of sake and who the mastermind was behind the concept of letting rice ferment to make an alcoholic beverage, historians have successfully dated sake's roots to 500 B.C. in China, before the rice was locally grown for sake in Japan.

People spat chewed rice together. The more people that came to spit chewed rice, the larger the amount of sake was brewed to be enjoyed by all. People always linked their bond with the Shinto Gods with sake. Given the importance now, the villagers then decided to let the virgin females in the community contribute to the making of sake by chewing and spitting in the hope of appeasing the gods more, as virgins were the purest of all. This sprouted the brewing of sake as more and more people were attracted to the intoxicating beverage, known as Bijinshu. With time as Bijinshu (female virgins spitting rice for sake brewing) was practiced more and more, it became a festivity where communities would gather in large number to celebrate and rejoice the making of sake until it reached the ears of the upper class in their society till Imperial Court in Japan. It was then, as sake started to be brewed for festivities, did the Japanese call it the Minzoku No Sake, meaning sake that is brewed for a catered reason rather than accidental discovery. It was then that the local communities continued to use rice until it led to the birthing of a new sake, or Nihonshu.

The buoyant celebration of the farmers led to rising curiosity in the upper societies residing in the Imperial Court. They wanted to know what was it that made the farmers happy and how they came about it. Once the higher classes discovered sake, they were adamant about improving the quality and taste of the sake to differentiate it from the sake consumed by the commoners. It was all a matter of class segregation. The Imperial Court ordered the brewers to develop a method of production that would be different, leading to the discovery of Koji. This breakthrough led to complete eradication of the olden chewing and spitting method of sake brewing and naturally required for tools to be enhanced. The brewers grew intrigued during the beginning of the Nara period in the 7th century. How they could have variants of sake, they wanted to play more with different ingredients and techniques to see the results they could yield. Only the confinement of the Imperial Court bothered the brewers, as sake made there was solely for the elites. Sake turned into a monopoly for the rich, holding back all those who wanted to expand their own pool of knowledge.

Mass brewing in the 10th and distilleries in the 13th Century

With the will to expand their breweries and have control over it, these brewers ventured into other temples and shrines within neighboring districts. The reason these brewers chose temples and shrines for sake brewing was the abundant supply of water that the temples controlled, and the dedicated monks who were willing to work as a laborer for the production, as they believed sake was the drink of the Gods. Brewers by now had learned how water played a crucial role in the varying texture of sake, and temples were constructed in places with an abundance of optimal water.

As the brewers continued to meddle with the ingredients, newer techniques evolved too that soon replaced the traditional chew-and-spit method. Brewers had learned how water content changes fermentation, amongst these new methods, was the Bodai Moto technique. In this, the brewers decided to add airborne yeast to a large amount of water, infusing it into the rice before the mixture was placed into a vat to ferment. This new method resulted in a sour sake brew than ever before.

The monks continued to experiment with various techniques as they diligently worked on crafting a mold that would ease the break-down process of starch into glucose that would aid them if the rice were polished. Hence, they birthed the concept of polished rice that advanced with time. While the brewers and monks worked day and night to refine sake, they still faced a threat where sake had a limited shelf-life.

During one of these amazing evolutions, pasteurization came long before the Frenchman made his discovery known. Brewers in Japan realized if they were to heat the sake concoction after it was made, it would allow for the drink to be preserved for a longer period of time. With this, more and more brewers were encouraged to try something new with the techniques and ingredients in the hopes of yielding better results than their competitors, while also producing a unique formula of sake. There was a constraint, nonetheless. As brewers who had set up ventures were located in districts where shrines and temples were, these brewers wanted to go back home to where their families were, hence birthing more distilleries throughout Japan.

Kudari-Zake in the 1700s

Sake brewing bloomed during the Edo period. While Kyoto and Kobe were areas with the most breweries due to the water springs there, smaller brewers made way for their own villages, where they prompted the possibility of sake brewing for their community. A fine line was created where the larger breweries catered supplies for distant cities, while small breweries catered to their local population within the villages. Meanwhile, affluent Edo (Tokyo) residents preferred sake brewed in Nada and called it a Kudari-zake.

The high involvement of the community was once more used to produce sake. It was given that farmers were idle throughout winters as they had to wait until spring to reap their crops. Later on, brewers had discovered the best time to brew sake was in winter due to the amount of yeast produced by it's neutralizing effect on the hot fermentation period. It was during the Edo period where brewers discovered the Kimoto process of making yeast starters, thus eliminating the dependency on airborne yeast to break down glucose into alcohol.

The more the brewers played around with the process of fermentation, water, and now koji yeast, the more they grew inquisitive to discover new methods that would aid them in the production of sake. As a result, this was the era when brewers discovered the usage of distilled alcohol to be added to the sake concoction and the use of waterwheels. The monks had long discovered if they were to remove the bran from the rice, it would speed up the process of fermentation. Now brewers wanted to speed up the process more, leaving them to rely on the usage of waterwheels.

Brewers worked day and night to ensure the smooth production of sake, which resulted in a symbolic move for Japan as people brought their ceramic jugs to be filled with sake. Toward the end of the cycle, sake was spotted being in glass bottles, a major breakthrough in the entire process of sake development.

Meiji Restoration

It was known how popular and cherished sake was for Japan. It was not only a great opportunity for newer businesses and the creation of more jobs but also an opportunity for the government to regulate the entire production of sake to ensure quality while earning taxes from it. Laws were made, encouraging people to start their own brewery and to be of advantage for the rich. While there were nearly 30,000 breweries initially, only 8,000 were left due to biased laws that favored larger breweries. The sake industry was booming, and this led to the commercialization of the drink. After all, this was what had scaled up the production of sake back at the Imperial Court. Naturally, larger breweries were at an advantage compared to the smaller ones.

The government encouraged anyone with money and materials to operate their own business. The affluent brewers were able to brand their sake, making it the desired choice for consumers as they were the ones with wider access to the market for raw materials. The more a smooth-running brewery gained business, the more they were able to influence the market, putting smaller breweries out of business.

20th Century Evolution

Larger breweries could ship their sake to the furthest ends of Japan, while smaller breweries were left to watch in vain. What was once an elixir of celebration and joy became a fight for survival among breweries. The Treasury created a National Research Institute of Breweries to help sake brewers, yet it was only the rich who gained the most benefits. After this initiative was successful, the Treasury went on in partnership with Japan sake brewers to form another body – the National New Sake Competition. This was a government-funded competition that tasted the sake produced. The verdict imposed dictated which sake was to be purchased by consumers.

On one hand, the partnership of the government with the Sake Association brought sake making to an international level where sake was now prominent in Japan. On the other hand, it created a fine line of tension among businesses as people wanted the most verified and perfected form of sake. As competition heightened, it led to a stronger need for new technological advancements. Soon, water wheels were replaced with polishing machines, variants of concentrated yeasts were available in markets, and the old wooden vats were replaced with larger and proper enamel tanks that did not affect the after-taste of sake. The finer mesh was available to ensure the even and smooth production of sake. Smaller breweries were left to fend for themselves with traditional methods of brewing sake and had less business compared to their high-scale competitors. The time taken by smaller businesses to ferment sake was equivalent to the time larger breweries had to put their bottles of sake available on the market.

The government promoted the usage of enamel tanks over the wooden barrels with the claim that the tanks were easier to maintain. This instantly placed smaller breweries at a disadvantage as they were unable to afford enamel tanks and the government-induced higher taxation of enamel tanks. The more tanks were used, the more tax-revenue was generated, leading to the end of smaller and home-based sake breweries.

As more modernized methods evolved, older methods such as the Kimoto method faced a threat. Naturally, the Kimoto process was tedious, leading the brewers to develop the Yamahai method that made yeast starters easier to develop. The other process was known as Sokujo-Moto.

This involved the addition of lactic acid to the sake concoction that worked alongside yeast as a catalyst to speed up the fermentation process. As more well-established breweries flourished, the more they contributed to the tax revenue. In 1898 alone, the government earned a total of five million yen in tax from sake, which was 4.6% of their direct income tax.

It seemed as if the sake business were reaching new milestones. It was a seamless run until the wave of the Great Depression hit Japan. The very few home-based breweries that existed were unable to withstand the aftermath of the Great Depression and were put out of business completely. There was a need for the rice to be eaten rather than drank as many were starving.

With wars and the Great Depression, most of the rice grown was sent for consumption than to breweries. This was a challenge that determined the fate of the existing breweries as they had to improvise a way to ensure that sake was just as good. This was when breweries resorted to the addition of distilled alcohol to the sake concoction. Brewers realized that by having added distilled alcohol, they multiplied the amount of their batch threefold, naming the sake produced in such a way as *Sambai Zojoshu*. It became a common practice that helped brewers fight even the harshest of weather to ensure they would remain in business.

In time, breweries continued to turn for the worst and left some of the oldest breweries in Japan to file for bankruptcy when Japan was at war with China. Once more, the need for the rice to be eaten exceeded the need to drink sake. Once one war was over, another began. During WWII, the government had completely overtaken businesses, controlling what and how much they produced. The result was that from the tens of thousands of breweries, there were barely 3,000 breweries left nationwide that successfully continue to produce sake even to this date.

The state of sake now

One thing that amazes me is how sake never stopped evolving. At the same time, sake requires four basic ingredients that have been around since the very beginning – rice, water, Koji enzymes, and yeast. After 1945, as Japan rebuilt its damaged infrastructure and economy, so did sake breweries. They continued to modernize their production methods. Throughout all these procedures, sake still had a distinct texture and aroma, from coarse to chunky and opaque textures. From having either a very sour taste to a sweet and bitter taste. The variants were endless, and brewers continuously tried with the new procedures and production of sake.

They did not want sake to have a syrup-like consistency. Sake was not always a clean, crisp, and light drink that adorned frosted glass bottles. It was dense and sturdy, all of which were changed with modernization. Each district had its preference that they adhered to at times as well as improvised. A few districts polished their rice to more than 20%, all of which was done to gain the approval from National Sake Appraisal. These sake breweries would produce a drink that was light, succulent, and eloquent. In short, this sake transformed into a refined drink that was quick to gain the attention of the entire industry and government, marking the boom in production of the Ginjo and Daiginjo.

Such sake was loved by all, enticing people into the procedure of milling and polishing rice grains before using them. Soon a category was set up as brewers continued to reduce the size of rice grain. People did not want to pay the same amount for each sake when each was made differently. With categorization, it enabled both brewers and consumers with the benefit to not only identify their favorite sake brew but also to pay for the amount of labor involved.

This contributed to the three categories of distinguishing sake: ingredients used, brewing process, and after-treatment. Ingredients determined how the rice was treated and to what extent, e.g., the percentage of rice milled. The brewing process determined if the methods were Kimoto/Yamahai or Sukojo. The last became the after-treatment, such as if the sake was pasteurized or filtered to identify the end product.

The government-led effort to standardize sake labeling system also led brewers to rush toward the classification system and to have their sake labeled accordingly. Consumers were willing to pay the varying prices, even when sake prices rocketed up due to the efforts brewers were putting in. This labeling system enabled brewers to demand higher prices, while consumers enjoyed crisper and cleaner sake than the previous robust versions.

The Ginjo movement birthed the introduction to *Premium Sake* and *Table Sake*. Subsequently, while there were only 3,000 breweries competing for production, after the Ginjo movement, only 1,400 managed to survive. These surviving breweries today are further classified as the major brewers and the microbrewers known as Jizake in the local market. Now, if you think the microbrewers are producing ordinary sake, then you are mistaken. These Jizake are the ones who make specially crafted premium sake, while the major breweries produce table sake befitting everyday consumption.

Some prefer their sake to be strong, while some prefer it to be light. Some wish for fruity notes while some for an acidic taste. Sake has genuinely evolved with time and is a drink appreciated globally.

Chapter 6
Toji, Kuramoto, Kurabito, and Machine Learning

A system of crafting

How was Sake shaped to be what we know it to be today? The answer to this lies within the Toji's, Kurabito's, and Kuramoto's, whose hard work has brought forth sake for us to indulge in. I would like to share some insight with you to help you understand something about Japanese society and illustrate how their society works.

I have found a great contrast – to be both an American citizen and a Japanese citizen. It is a completely different experience. I was born in Osaka, Japan, a Japanese national by birth. Only during the late '80s while I was in New York did I become a green card holder that came from winning the immigration lottery.

In the late-'90s, I moved to San Francisco. None of my family in Japan ever wanted to migrate to the United States. Up to this day, none of my relatives ever expressed any interest moving to San Francisco. I think no one wants to venture outside of their comfort zone unless it's needed for any extreme reason. Did I really need to be in New York City? To simply put it, there was little need for me to be in the U.S. Rather, I just wanted to challenge the norm by forcing myself to leave my comfort zone and challenge the status quo. Why? I grew up with a lot of Japan-born Koreans that often told me that it's impossible to overcome the status quo and I was always curious to see if they were right.

During my immigration period, the economy was doing extremely well in Japan. I remember some of my friends in the advertising industry in Japan telling me to head back home, "What are you doing in New York? Come back home and work on a real project!" Back then, I was working on projects for a large advertising agency. Working in the advertising industry around that time was a treat; Every day was a party. My instructor from the art college that I was attending had hired me as a paid intern at first, then as a full-time employee. During my time there, I used to consume a massive amount of alcohol while partying with renowned copywriters, art directors, photographers and illustrators and after work. I recalled no one ever ordered Sake, even at the priciest of bars and restaurants in town.

Prior to the BRC, a.k.a. the Burning Man event, David, the head at the Camp Synthesis, had asked me to post recruitment information of his camp at a Japanese Burner Facebook group page. I translated the introduction David provided me with into Japanese before posting it on a couple of Facebook group pages, as the camp was lacking female members.

Two of the Japanese theme camps at the BRC had nearly 200 participants who flew in from Japan just to attend the Burning Man Event. Over there, I met with a person named Nao that signed up for the duty prior to coming to the event. He was one of the participants of the Step in Life camp that had the theme of the Shinto Shrine Summer Festival. Yeah, Shinto again.

I had to drive to the BRC on my own, as the rest of the campers left earlier. It seems to me that there are always unforeseen problems lurking around and that I needed someone else to watch over me, who would not sleep on the wheel. If I were to recruit an American who can't afford their own transportation, it would have been a risk, in my opinion. I had to recruit a person from Japan to do the duty by thinking that at least they were able to afford their airplane ticket.

One thing that I found to be rather peculiar was that all of the campers were strangers at this Japanese theme camp, as well as the camp I was attending. There were nearly 10 people, all of whom were Japanese guys, yet not one of them had brought sake but, their Taiwanese friends had some sake in their camp.

Most Japanese burners could barely converse in English, while the Taiwanese burners were mostly fluent in Mandarin, Japanese, and English. This was enough to affirm my fear of sake, which is a long-lost tradition in Japan that is symbolized by the Japanese youth not taking much more risks detaching themselves from their norm.

The organizers of the camp had a playa name Tencho (store manager.) The organizer was an engineer at a Robotics company in Tokyo, that develops the Takoyaki Robot. His camp was operating Takoyaki stands. This camp was well-organized compared to other camps I'd seen thus far in the BRC. Yet, he didn't charge his campers extra to rent an RV for himself.

Toji

This is one aspect I am talking about as the difference between Americans and Japanese. How the head of the organization in the U.S. makes 100 times more money than their lower end of employees? A Japanese man who makes a smart system integrates himself within the ecosystem he has created that overlooks him not being compensated 100 times more than his employees. This is the same for Toji.

Then the question is why the Japanese don't care about money? This was from an old Japanese sentiment that people care more about honor instead. The Shogun in the Edo period came up with a rigid social caste system that stopped anybody from accumulating too much financial fortune to avoid any uprisings.

Sake brewing has been a traditional industry since the beginning of time and has a proper brewer system. There are only a handful of such people involved in the sake brewing process, who, after enduring years of experience, acquire the requisite skills to be a Toji. Toji, a hands-on manager that overlooks and disciplines all of the processes of sake brewing. Toji possesses all the skills of the chief executive in the company. The cultivated culture of the special craftsman was delicately nurtured throughout Japan's districts and regions, forming a craftsman group and establishing a renowned, nationwide discharge area.

The Japanese are rarely terminated by their employers. They work in a system called Nenko Joretsu, the seniority-wage system. This Japanese system of promoting staff in compliance with their retirement, senior employees benefit in that they are offered a higher salary package as per their expertise and experience, while also elevating their rank, thus gaining more benefits from the company.

Such employees prefer to stay within the company until they retire, hence the benefit for both the employees and the employer. While this act develops a sense of loyalty within the employees, it helps the employer reap the benefits of their senior-most executive's expertise.

This is the role of a Toji in sake brewing. The person who receives the title of Toji after years of working and hands on experience that benefits the sake brewers. It is an essential give-and-take, where one party gets paid as per their experience, and the other reaps the benefits of their senior-most executive's expertise in sake making.

Kuramoto

Kuramoto plays the management's role in the sake brewery. They are the ones who get to strategize and plan. They determine the type of liquor to be produced, highlight the company's weaknesses and strengths, what should be brought up, and what should be eliminated. The Kuramoto is the general producer of the company in the hopes of keeping the business running seamlessly and successfully while assessing risk management.

Kurabito

A Kurabito is a craftsman who brews sake. There is an assistant known as the Kashira or "the head assistant". There are Kojishi and are solely responsible for making Koji. There are the Motochiri, who look after the making of sake and direct the brewers in charge of each process differently. Furthermore, there are Usuya's who manage the rice milling work in breweries where they mill their own sake rice. There are breweries who outsource their work as well. With professionals, the brewers come together to reap the benefits of their skills and knowledge to produce a sake that is succulent.

What is Toji's responsibility?

Toji's are the maestro and the captain of the brewery where Kurabito takes orders from and obey 100%. These are the men who have not only acquired skills over time but also mastered their art to precision before they are allowed to play with the tantalizing taste of sake. They produce a fine selection for us, but even Toji aims to think about what the brewery wants as a whole. For the Kimoto-style sake brewing, the Toji and Kurabito stay in their Kuramoto for about 6 months from fall to spring. From being seasonal work for farmers during the off-season to the winters, farmers that would be waiting for their crops to grow would find extra work in sake brewing.

It is known that the rice-growing season in Japan lasts from Spring to Autumn. Now, it is practically all-year-round. From then onward, it was observed that farmers who religiously partook in the position of sake brewers were far better and well-versed with the entire process as opposed to the new farmers joining every year.

Ever since the concept of a Toji was developed, these were the men known for bringing back a failing sake to its prime. Along the lines of the brewing process, there were setbacks faced as well, such as rice solubility and finding the right amount of starch required. This introduced the dire need of a Toji, as they were the problem-solvers. This was where the farmers stepped in and used their skills to use other than being rice farmers.

There came a decline in maestros of sake, and the need to have such masters became crucial. Hence, the Tojis came forth not only to offer their skills, but to also teach the new-age sake enthusiasts and fanatics to be a Toji. The Tojis are the reason why you always find the best and unique sake, and that is the very reason why breweries only hire one Toji. Yes, only one! This practice allows each master to offer their wizardry and produce a taste that is unique to their brewery.

Not everyone can become a Toji. They need to be accredited enough before applying for the position in a brewery. The standard to become one is by joining a Sakagura or sake brewery. Just like in any other job before you come to the position of an executive, you need to join your field and work there. Similarly, to be a Toji, you need to work as a sake brewer and gain enough experience before getting an offer to be a Toji.

With time, there came a drastic need for the guild of Tojis, as they needed to train new sake brewers. Thus, it led to the birth of various Toji schools. There are different schools of Toji and divided up by region, and practises its own unique brand of sake brewing.

Toji Schools

The farmers who used to outsource their skills during off-season saw how their knowledge was sought after, leading them to offer their skills to the guilds. These guilds started to associate with the farmers and managed the entire process of extending their services to the brewers. With time, these associations also started to see a rise of interested and keen sake brewers who wanted to learn from the very Tojis. This soon gave way to the Toji Guild era, where there was at least one association in every region, except for Tokyo. During the peak of this era, a few associations even bore witness to over 1,000 associates and at least a hundred Tojis.

In due time and as of today, there are numerous Toji associations still present now known as Toji Schools and they all practice and perfect a blend native to their region. Among the many schools, the most major ones are:

Nanbu Toji

Despite the fact that the number of Tojis has decreased, Nanbu Toji is Japan's biggest Toji group, which originated in the Kitakawami basin of the Iwate prefecture. Presently, it is situated in Ishidoriya-Cho, Hanamaki-shi.

Echigo Toji

Echigo Toji is native to the mid-southern part of the Niigata prefecture and was once the biggest Toji in Japan. As the Niigata is the home of the most number of breweries in Japan, they all have Tojis from Echigo Toji.

Tanba Toji

The Tanba Toji is native to Tanba-Sasayama City in the Hyogo prefecture, and was raised by the breweries in the Nada region. It is well-known for crafting most of the meishu (a fame sake brand) and was once the largest association. It went further than any other guild across Japan to instruct and guide the different regions in devising a prototype for a regional sake.

These three Tojis are accredited, and are the topmost in Japan, they are known as the sandai-toji-shudan (three major toji groups). Alas, these guilds are losing themselves with time. Their concept of persuasions has mostly faded and leaving persuasions as more of a structure with less people participating.

The present situation of toji

Understanding how the culmination of a Toji is developed over time and passed down from one Toji to another, it is no shock that the special knowledge of Tojis is slowly diminishing. The lack of Tojis resulted the existing ones being expensive to hire, most breweries have decided to proceed with their business without a Toji.

To top it all off, sake is losing its popularity in Japan, as the younger population is no longer interested enough or just apathetic towards the drink to learn more about its rich history. The decline of Toji schools is also caused by the younger population's disinterest in learning to master the art of sake brewing. As a result, Toji masters no longer have a grand pool of students to pass their skills down to. This greatly threatens the art and mastery of sake brewing, as there are no newer associates willing to learn the skill.

The cost of keeping up with the industry is another hindrance. While the younger generation deems sake to be outdated, marketers are injecting more capital in the packaging that burdens their overall cost, further adding to the price the consumers have to pay. But is the younger generation willing to pay for a bottle of sake that costs more than beer? Sadly, the answer is no. People are comparing sake to other alcoholic beverages from around the world. The brewers are left to tackle problems such as a lack of labor and the rising cost of keeping up with the current market, endangering more and more breweries to go out of business. Such a depiction vindicates how the practice of being a Toji is now being lost. The need for having an intellectual who had the experience, to focus on skills being enhanced within breweries, the concept and era of Toji are no longer a necessity to sake brewing.

Dassai Computing Sake

Coming to understand how brewers prefer enhancing their production rather than to solely rely on the concept of a Toji, one of Japan's most famous companies resorted to a modern uptake on their production. It is none other than the creators of Dassai Sake. In collaboration with the Dassai Sake owned by Asahi Shuzo Brewery and Fujitsu, the brewery was able to brew Dassai sake based on Artificial Intelligence's (AI) to uplift. They believe that AI can integrate mathematical components to remodel and redefine sake brewing with machinery, having gathered data from the original Dassai process that was created by a Toji that fled from his duty.

Dassai always envisioned sake to be a brew that is sipped and enjoyed rather than gulped down for the sheer purpose of sales. They always paid attention to the details, and that led them to be amongst the top brewers in Japan. Using the same keen interest, Dassai is among the first few to realize the decline of the Tojis and Kurabitos, leading them to generate the usage of data in the brewing process. Having the best interest of the company in mind and to combat the issues at hand, Asahi brewery wished to improve the quality of Dassai with the minimum amount of laborers in his breweries. What better than AI to rely on for this?

Over the years, Dassai has been quick to record and store their data. Each process the brewery goes through requires precision. Dassai had already deployed Fujitsu's IT technology to farms that cultivate Yamadanishiki, the rice requisite for sake brewing, in the hopes of systematizing and acquiring agricultural data for the best sake rice farming. With the same idea in mind, Dassai wishes to apply this fully to their entire brewing process.

With this initiative, Dassai and Fujitsu aspired to harbor information that supports the sake brewing by calculating the predicted information and gauging the optimal control settings that are the best for sake brewing. Furthermore, they wish to enhance their work efficiency and improve the productivity of the entire brewing process. They are doing this by offering readability and a comprehensive display of the AI's predictions. This way, everyone would be able to understand the computed data and what is best for the sake brewing in each category.

With all of the data that the AI has to gather, Fujitsu further offers Dassai easier means to compute their data for better utilization by retaining the previous insights of Dassai. With the AI that Dassai aims to use, they will be able not only to be able to preserve the precise methods that are used to practice for the optimum sake, but they are also able to use the biological statistics for defining their processes, such as fermentation. All of this to be able to control their sake brewing process digitally, giving way to a sophisticated and intricately detailed framework that aided Dassai in concocting premium sake.

Machine Learning and Sake

Back in BRC, Tencho's Takoyaki stand is operated by 100% human laborers, while his robots make Takoyakis in Tokyo at a pace that meets with the market's demand while lowering production costs. It made me wonder if robots are also capable of brewing sake if the process can be computed this way. The initiative Dassai is taking with Fujitsu to turn this idea into reality. If they are to obtain the desired data from the current labor-intensive procedure, Dassai can equip robots that can scan the data, pinpoint the precise temperature, the requisite amount of water, and the optimum amount of yeast to bring out the desired flavor of sake without the assistance of a Toji.

Along the line, the brewery that the sake tasting room in Berkeley doesn't have a Toji, but they do have a semi-automated process that the humans oversee and assist in tasks that need to be done manually.

Aramasa Brewery IT system

There is a brewery named Aramasa in the Akita prefecture that started its operations in 1700. The current owner, who is the great, great-grandson of the founder, has started brewing sake by using 96% polished off the rice. Up until his experiment, a lot of people asked: "Can you brew sake with 100% unpolished rice?" It is possible, but difficult to manage in the fermentation process.

At Aramasa, they are experimenting with their brewing of sake by using yeast number six with 96% polished off the rice. The head of the company, also a Toji, uses an in-house, state-of-art IT system to analyze a sample of the fermentation. They monitor the fermentation process with an electronic microscope to see how the microbes proliferate.

This is the segment that I think they can incorporate and use machine learning instead of analyzing data through human eyes. I deem it to be more efficient to be understanding data via the laboratories as analysis can be a deep learning neural network for making the best available decisions.

After all, what a Toji does is that they exploit historical data to gain insight on what to do with their sake. If a brewery wants to explore new possibilities, using neural networks for regression, classification, with unstructured data can make things more accurate, faster, and easier for any untrained brewers, the sake industry will improve their quality so that they can reach markets in or outside of Japan. Dassai wants to win trust over its high-quality sake in the U.S.

Chapter 7
Kikisake-Shi: Sake Sommelier

Silicon Valley and winery

I started my sake journey based on this fact: I unintentionally lost my full-time job every one to three years. It is a popular trend in the high-tech industry, people never stay with one company for longer than 2 years. After 2 years, your skills stall and won't be able to transfer it to the new jobs. Again, sake and Burning Man weren't what I had planned to take any interest in, I only wanted to get connected with the high-tech industry and its people.

It was only after I worked in the sake tasting room doing a sommelier type of job, I found myself quite good at it. As a matter of fact, my performance is getting 5-star ratings on yelp from the elite yelpers. Before we start talking about sake sommeliers, I wish to create a bridge for you to be able to better understand what Kikisake-shi or Sake Sommelier means.

My first encounter with a sommelier was about eight years ago when I was hired to videotape the very first bottling for a winery in Napa Valley. The owner of the winery was the founder and former CEO of a well-established video game company in Silicon Valley and is originally from Osaka. Kenzo, the CEO, retired to open his own winery in Napa after he made a fortune. Over there, I worked with a Japanese sommelier from Tokyo that he hired to consult on how to price Kenzo's wine.

This must be a part of the Silicon Valley success story; Many entrepreneurs sold their startups and cashed out their stock options to buy their own winery. In fact, I had met another man who had done what Kenzo did. He was the founder of popular bookkeeping software, and had sold his business to a Fortune 100 company, then started his own winery.

I will sidetrack a little bit more, divulging into what I learned from my documentary video gig in Napa. A couple of weeks before the Burning Man Event, an American sommelier working for a winery in Napa with her two friends came to the sake tasting room. She had come to the tasting room for her exam certification that required knowledge on sake, hence leading her to the tasting room. She had to do a research summary, and this is how I had gotten the chance to meet with her. Throughout the interaction, I discovered how interesting the experience was, it is a wholesome and enriching journey where one person is educating everyone on sake.

It led me to wonder how these people could be consultants to breweries, helping them with pricing sake. It also led me to think the same can be achieved by Machine Learning as well. For instance, AI can not only come up with the product, e.g., wine/sake, but can also suggest the optimal location, timing, and food for the wine/sake to be consumed with.

AI can also suggest the quantity of sake to be produced and would take that into it's pricing consideration. Based on these suggestions, AI can then help wine sommeliers price their product justly, as per the location of serving, timing, and the food to be consumed. My journey surely had been an enriching one, during which I realized a change in a pattern where people came together with sommeliers in a coffee house kind of setting to learn about the art of breweries and become a sommelier themselves. In the end, it is interesting how human opinion can be so accurate. With this, I realized during my video gig in Napa, where I found myself asking the same question to the sommelier. He explained to me how it all depends on the reputation of a sommelier, which is based on years of experience.

The sommelier culture is from Europe, but to be a sake sommelier, there are some criteria that an individual needs to satisfy to be qualified. As it turns out to be, you can become a well-rounded sake sommelier if you are a Toji. Even an American Toji can have people agreeing, as chief sake can price sake more than its volume. Only, for sake, the sommeliers are known as Kikisake-Shi.

Kikisake-Shi

What is a Kikisake-Shi? If you are to google Kikisake-Shi, you will come across various definitions like, "a professional who is certified and equipped with enough knowledge to provide or sell sake in various languages that are native to their target country or audience." By this, you must have already understood that a Kikisake-Shi is a person of immense value. Of course, such value is gained through efforts. To be a Kikisake-Shi, you must be certified after passing many examinations and having the requisite experience.

There is more to what a Kikisake-Shi is than the standard definition provided by a search engine; It is more than just a title a person earns based on paper-merit. It is rather a title gained based on one's palate from my perspective. Generally, I found that if someone introduced themselves as a Kikisake-Shi, people around them would be amused and intrigued as have I.

A Kikisake-Shi is a person of importance, and you can rely on the expertise they have established after years of sake tasting and understanding to help you either make a selection or to learn a thing or two about sake. It is a title that impresses people, yet most people call a Kikisake-Shi to be a sake sommelier. A Kikisake-Shi is more than just a sommelier. The term actually translates to tasting sake, and the Shi refers to a professional. They are the maestros and can be sake fanatics, helping the sake fandom and people like me who wish to learn about sake.

The Kikisake-Shi's are people especially qualified to render their services to the food and beverage industry, helping the industry with pricing and volumes to be produced, while aiding the consumers with pairing suggestions and different tastes a bottle of sake has to offer. They do not only educate people about the tones and flavors present in a sake bottle but also delight people with the history, culture, and production process of sake, henceforth providing them with a fulfilling experience and expanding their knowledge.

Having learned about from the types of sake to its production methods, it is safe to say that sake is a complex drink that new drinkers can not comprehend. Thus, in such cases, we need professional help, and this is where Kikisake-Shi steps in. If not for them, most of the people may not even enjoy sake, for they may have chosen a concoction that does not suit their taste buds. Kikisake-Shis are an integral part of the sake industry and why they rely on them. But can anyone be a Kikisake-Shi?

How to Be a Kikisake-Shi?

While many people hope to attain the prestigious title of a Kikisake-Shi, not everyone can handle the responsibility or perform the duty of a Kikisake-Shi correctly. Furthermore, with the widespread awareness and demand for sake around the globe, the standards to be a Kikisake-Shi have now heightened as well.

Now there are professional examination courses available that sake enthusiasts, sommeliers, and even Toji masters can take to become a connoisseur. Usually, these courses are conducted by SSI International. Once a person clears the examination, they are awarded a certification of international credibility to be a Kikisake-Shi.

At the moment, the SSI International only conducts the test in a limited range of languages that include English, Chinese, French, Spanish, and Korean. However, if a person, for example, wishes to take the test in Korean, they would be required to register themselves at Soongsil University in Korea, where proper lectures are conducted before a person can sit for their exam. The exam comprises an array of questions, which cover topics from basic sake history, ingredients used in different sakes, brewing method, production method, questions to evaluate sake tasting, how sake should be served, and sake labeling.

In short, any question associated with sake can be asked, leaving the people that are taking the challenge to study through a plethora of textbooks. The process is tedious, which is why if a person is certified to be a Kikisake-Shi, they usually are competent and hard to become one of them.

Skills of a Kikisake-Shi

One may study and memorize all facts of sake, even unearth the most uncommon knowledge, yet a person can fail to be a good Kikisake-Shi. Then what makes a person believe that they can take the responsibility of a Kikisake-Shi? I will be listing a few qualities that even the SSI International seeks in their students, apart from focusing solely on their academic results before they can award an individual with the international certificate of being a Kikisake-Shi.

Number One: An individual has to be insightful

A Kikisake-Shi is supposed to help customers evaluate a drink based on their preference. Hence, if they cannot see through or understand their customer's needs, they will not be able to sell the desired product to the customer.

Number Two: They need to be passionate about hospitality

This is one of the most crucial requirements. We understand that every person is different in nature – some are introverts, some extroverts, and others ambiverts. To be a Kikisake-Shi, a person needs to love people, their job, as well as accept the prospect of approaching people. They need to be hospitable toward their customers in order to successfully sell sake, because if they are not able to, then they may scare customers off. To be a Kikisake-Shi, it is required to interact with people, and if a Kikisake-Shi is not approachable, they will fail at their job.

Number Three: They should be able to retain all information about sake

This is of absolute significance to being a Kikisake-Shi. A Kikisake-Shi needs to be well-versed in every aspect of the drink, from how ingredients contribute to the flavor, to where the ingredients were from and how they were cultivated. Even the history of sake is of the essence, and a Kikisake-Shi needs to know all of this at all times. Each and every bit of knowledge should be dispensable to a Kikisake-Shi all the time. How will a customer feel if they ask a Kikisake-Shi for their expertise, but they fail in answering the question because they don't know? It would be embarrassing. Thus, it is important for all Kikisake-Shi to know everything about sake.

Number Four: They need to understand each type of sake and how the pairing is done with food

The reason people seek Kikisake-Shi is for their information. Their information is not limited to just the geographical, historical, and production aspects of sake. They should also know the effects sake can have on the body and what sort of after-taste they produce when consumed with a type of food. Their knowledge and understanding about the process of sake liquor interacting with food to produce a certain taste should be vast in order to guide a consumer thoroughly.

Number Five: They need to be expert in sake

This point is a reassertion of the points above, meaning it is of high importance that a Kikisake-Shi is equipped with all information on sake at all times. They should know more than their customers and need to be able to answer all queries about sake. Having all of this information certifies an individual to be a Kikisake-Shi.

Number Six: Skills

Not everyone can adapt to the contrasting flavors present in sake, let alone understand them. To be a Kikisake-Shi, the student needs to be able to understand the flavors of sake and how much should be served. They even have to think about how the kind of serving glass affects the taste of the drink drastically. Hence, a Kikisake-Shi should understand their liquor in-and-out. They portray their skills of tasting sake explicitly in order to help consumers, be it for pricing or selling. They also are able to compare two sakes and highlight the correct taste and production methods used to justify the pricing of sake.

Number Seven: They should be able to pitch proposals

Here comes the fun and challenging part of being a Kikisake-Shi. Understanding that these people help brewers to price their sake, they also all need to have one important skill in them – to be able to sell their words. If a Kikisake-Shi sounds confused, nervous, or unconvinced about the sake they are pitching, no consumer will take their verdict seriously. A good Kikisake-Shi should have great interpersonal communication skills. They need to be able to pitch proposals of breweries to a wider audience. They have to make their statement sound and as elaborate as possible. If they lack confidence, then having all of the information about sake will be of no use.

Responsibilities of a Kikisake-Shi

Well, if one wishes to take this challenge, they need to be responsible for the following:

Offer a good range of sake in its best form

Having been told how a Kikisake-Shi is to provide and sell sake, they only gain credibility and good rapport if they are able to offer the best sake possible. For that, they need to evaluate a sake fully, meaning from its brewing process to tones before they can market the bottle. Amidst the process, the Kikisake-Shis are to achieve the rightful qualification and be experienced tasters that will help them identify a bottle that offers a stale test so as not to sell it to the consumers. If they cannot identify the bad from the good, then who else will?

Understand the tones of sake and what food they should be paired with

The one aspect of being a Kikisake-Shi that enchants me is how they understand the depths of the flavor present in a given bottle of sake. It is a crucial understanding that a good Kikisake-Shi should know. SSI International ensures this is tested before they issue a certificate to an individual, proclaiming them to be an expert. In the testing, they divide the sake into four categories based on a taste that is taught to each student. Then the students are taught not only to identify the different four categories but also to understand each of them in detail to correlate them with the right food selection. Not every sake is meant to be enjoyed with every dish, but, it has to be carefully paired.

They should be able to explain each tone and flavor present in a bottle, even to a child

A Kikisake-Shi can remember every label on the bottles of sake. If you are to look at a label of a sake bottle, it will give you facts, though not very comprehensive. In the end, you might resort to asking a person working there to assist you in explaining what the words or ingredients on the label mean, but they only end up reading it word to word. It surely isn't helpful and would lead many to end their sake journey right there.

Now imagine the same scenario, but instead of asking anyone, you consult a Kikisake-Shi. These maestros will take the time to indulge you with all the information you desire. They will elaborate on the flavor and nature of the sake skillfully, illustrating the details that may take you to the fields in Japan, while keeping it simple enough to be understood by even a child.

Knowing their sake

Some of us may have experienced an incident whereby we ask for the background information of a product, but the person selling it may not possess the entire knowledge, leaving us confused about the product. As a result, we may not purchase it. So if a person wants to buy sake, but they are given inadequate information, they may be reluctant to make their purchase. In such a scenario, it is of utmost importance that the person selling or displaying a sake knows about each and every little detail of the beverage.

When asked, a Kikisake-Shi should be equipped with all knowledge on sake, including its history and brewery details at their fingertips. It is part of their prestige and honor, too, than to come off as an amateur.

Tips on Becoming a Kikisake-Shi

Once you ace your exams, your journey to sake learning does not end. You need to step out in the market and sell your skills to others for them to approach you for business. You can do so through the following methods:

Trust your taste buds

You need to understand your own taste buds first before you can comprehend the flavor of sake. You should also be able to tell if a sake has an off-taste and be able to point it out, despite what the brewers tell you. You need to trust in your taste buds so that others can trust your statement as well.

Focus on adjectives

You need to be friends with adjectives, as you will be using them repeatedly. Every sake will have multiple adjectives that you will need to introduce to your customers. Use them well and accurately in a way that would portray your skills and knowledge.

Practice all that you learn

When we learn something, our mind only retains the information for so long before it deems it to be idle and pushes it away at the back of our minds. In order for you to use all that you learn after your Kikisake-Shi course, you need to apply it to practical use. Apply all that you learn to your next placement of work.

Work for breweries and restaurants to gain more knowledge of sake

In order for you to be able to apply your learning, you need to work for breweries, restaurants, universities, and any other opportunity you are given. The fascinating part is that while you will be giving away your knowledge, you will be gaining new information in return. Every day in the practical field, you will encounter many scenarios and learn from them. The more you learn, the more proficient you will be as a Kikisake-Shi.

Interact with customers to understand their needs

You don't become a sake sommelier if you are unable to link your knowledge with the needs of your customers. Interact with people, ask them questions, find out what they are looking for and what they prefer. Only then can you offer the sake to them that befits their desires, as you cannot offer a complex sake to a new drinker.

How to Become a Successful Kikisake-Shi?
There are many sommeliers, some establish a successful

career for themselves, and some are unable to do so. So what contributes to the success of a sommelier then? It's simple: You have to stand out from your competition. For that, you can keep the following tips in mind that I have concluded for you, based on my experience thus far in my journey of sake exploration:

Be well versed with your drink

Do not think of being a Kikisake-Shi just as being a sommelier. Think through a marketing prospect as well. How do you market a product successfully and gain an advantage over your competitor? You need to understand your product in-and-out, in this case, your sake. This is why, during the Kikisake-Shi programs, students are taught as much as possible. Be it an individual customer, a brewer, or a restaurant, people will only approach you if you are well-versed with the information.

Know the selling point of your drinks and match it with the customer's preference

Gone are the days when sake was only in one pure form. There is now a wide variety of sake, from floral to fruity, opaque to clear, thick to thin liquid. There are mix-and-match and assorted sakes present. In order to gain the attention of your customers, ask them about their preferences. Do they wish to indulge in a lesser alcohol percentage? Do they have any specific sake in mind? Are they open to suggestions? Is this the first time they are having sake, or have they had sake before? Ask questions, any question about the customer's taste buds and likes, then offer them a sake that matches their tastes. This is a skill that is highly sought out after.

Be confident

They say confidence is beauty. That confidence is the key to attraction, and it's true. Confidence is what lets you stand out, it allows your personality to shine and is what attracts people to you. Confidence in a work setting is the soul of every product. You have to confidently make your statements and theories while you stand with your head high and a smile on your face. Your customers will be attracted to the confidence you display and will aid in your thriving career.

Have an impressive resume

Now that you have the certificate that proclaims you to be a Kikisake-Shi, you need to establish a clientele for yourself. People will not easily agree with your statements, even if they find your choices and suggestions of sake to be accurate. Therefore, use every opportunity that you get, big or small. Join every firm, every restaurant, and every brewery that you can to take for the experience. You will be surprised by just how much it will elevate your career.

Have fun

Work can be tiring. It often leaves us depleted of all energy. When we go for work the next day, the much needed enthusiasm is amiss. This imposes a threat to our image that we put forth for the perusal of others. No one likes a person who fails to find joy in their work, not even the person themselves. The work of a Kikisake-Shi, especially, lacks such enthusiasm since it can be repetitive in nature.

That being said, the one tip I consider to be the essence of all of this is to have fun. If you take work to be merely an occupation, with time, you will stop putting in the effort to make the most of your experience. Who says you cannot enjoy your work? In truth, if you turn your work into fun, you will wake up every day looking forward to it. Trust me, as a Kikisake-Shi, you will find that there is so much for you to enjoy, learn, and explore on a daily basis. All the free sake to taste, so never stop having fun.

Chapter 8
Sake, Sake Cocktails, & Food Pairing

Making your relationship more intimate

At the beginning of this book, I mentioned how I was mixing sake cocktails at the Burning Man. So what led me to mix cocktails there? It came from my observation of patrons of the tasting room and saw how they react to the traditional type of sake, Junmai sake, with a different umami taste. The patrons at the same time noted they like how the Daiginjo sake tastes. Although the Daiginjo sake is quite expensive as one bottle would easily cost $80, this was the kind of sake that everyone took a liking to immediately as one in ten tasting room visitors buy the Junmai Daiginjo sake.

Daiginjo sake tastes a little sweeter compared to other sake, like white wine. If you are wondering why the Daiginjo sake tastes sweeter as compared to Junmai sake for example is due to the process both types of sake undergo that affects the after-taste of the liquid. People found Junmai sake a little unusual as it contains higher umami or protein levels. It is during the fermentation process that the protein is converted into amino acids and glutamine, giving a little offset underlying taste. Daiginjo sake does not have this prominent protein-taste to it. This is why people identify their taste almost at the first sip, but then again the Daiginjo sake is pricier. Instead of offering the traditional sake or Daiginjo, I mixed unfiltered flavored sake with clear sparkling sake. As a result, 99% of them said, "Wow, this is amazing!" I knew what I had to do; thus, I came up with the concept of a sake-cocktail bar at the BRC without breaking my bank account.

I brought bottles of unfiltered sake and clear sparkling sake to my sake bar and served them on the first day. It was a hit. People craved more sake cocktails. This was where David, the organizer, came to me and said, "I have never seen people excited to drink sake before." So he decided to do the sake bar every night.

On the second day, I came up with an improvised sake cocktail, the 'sake of Manhattan', to preserve my supply for the next five days. I mixed plum flavored sake, Junmai sake, and Bourbon whiskey, then garnished the cocktail with Maraschino cherries. My idea was that the plum and Junmai sake would offer a sweet vermouth and bitter taste. Surprisingly, they worked even better than the original Manhattan cocktail. For the next day, I mixed Nigori sake with Pineapple flavored sake at a 1:1 ratio, and people loved it just as much.

While serving the cocktail of the day, I discovered another thing. The couples who came to my sake bar on the second day and beyond became very intimate after they had one or more cocktails. Now I have been to a few wine tasting rooms in Napa and Sonoma, but I do not see many people becoming intimate and kissing each other, unlike at my sake bar and also at the tasting sake room. I even thought of naming my cocktail, the 'Marriage Therapy Cocktail.'

Besides the cocktail, how to consume straight sake is a bit of a mystery because of the temperature of sake. Junmai Daiginjo sake for example is temperature sensitive and hence should be chilled. If we are serving a traditional Junmai sake or sake with distilled alcohol added to them, its liquid quality is not as exemplary. Mostly, these sakes are warmed at 95-120°F before consumption to alter the flavors just a little bit.

To Chill or Not to Chill

Should You Drink Sake at a Warm Temperature, Room Temperature, or Cold Temperature?

With all the sake hype going on, another thing that has taken quite a storm is the temperature. Is your sake served at the right temperature? You may often find a person who knows about sake to be arguing about the temperature of their sake. Should it be chilled or not? Should they be drinking it warm or chilled? It sounds bizarre when you think of it, but there is a deeper meaning behind this infamous argument, and I am here to guide you through it, so that the next time you hear someone arguing over the temperature of sake, you will be equipped with the right information to judge and settle it for the people. Long ago, when sake was brewed in tanks made out of cedar, they would turn out to be far denser, intense, sweet, and woody. This was why warming was best suited for the sake in the hopes of dulling such unrefined flavors. With time and as the brewing process changed, so did the temperature for sake. Newer strains were used that helped with refining the sake as much as possible. Different tanks were used for brewing and storage that had a weaker after-taste of wood and aroma. Even the yeast used changed with time, giving sake different profiles with varying fragrances and tastes. As a result, the desire to warm sake also altered.

Furthermore, with the addition of other ingredients such as fruity and floral essences, the sake gained a strong taste and scent. This results in a really eloquent and premium sake. If these liquids are heated, then the heat would break down the different tastes of sake, leading the drink to be bland. Understanding how heat was used in the olden days to mute the strong taste of sake, premium sake does not need to be heated anymore as it goes through various procedures that help tame the strong, original taste of sake. Now comes the truth in a nutshell: sake is to be enjoyed at various temperatures, one at which best defines the flavor.

The entire temperature debacle about sake is the bridge that allows the consumer to make the most of their drink. Not all sake are the same. Hence, a different temperature is best suited to each in the hopes of bringing out the maximum tones of the bottle.

Some sake are to be drunk at a lower temperature, and some at a warm temperature, but a harsh temperature will always destroy the taste of the sake. Sake placed at the wrong temperature can turn your sake to be either too subtle or too prominent. The temperature you drink your sake at is only to ensure that your drink offers you the most of its taste. Now that you understand the reason behind the importance of sake temperature, let's talk about the right temperature for different type of sakes.

Sake and Temperature

There is a famous myth around sake that a Premium Sake is best enjoyed chilled, and cheap sake is best enjoyed warmed. I want to clarify that this statement is nothing but false. It all depends on the type of sake as well as its flavor. Either temperature, cold or hot, leads to alteration in the flavor of the sake to bring out the best of it. Sometimes, chilling a sake can mute an undertone or two. Sometimes, heating a sake can elevate the different tones in a sake. Either way, there may be certain premium sakes that are consumed warm, some chilled, and some at a warmer temperature. Then what rule applies to determine the sake to associate it with its rightful temperature? Let's take a look at the very basics:

Cold Temperature

While some sake's are served chill,, it is never advised to overchill a sake. The reason for this is that if the drink is too cold, it will mute the entire taste of sake. From its aroma to the fruity or floral taste added, a cold sake will lose its flavor. The result will be a bitter sake.

On the other hand, if you simply chill a sake, it will offer you a clearer taste and a less umami flavor. The result will be a sake with a maximum fruity or floral scent that will be refreshing as you will slowly sip on your drink. Sakes are chilled when the brewer wants to offer the consumer a more floral or fruity taste. If the brewer wants to offer a richer taste and bring out the natural taste of the sake, then they advise the consumer to enjoy their drink warm.

Hot Temperature

The same goes for an overheated sake. The first thing a high temperature does is that it start to evaporate sake. Second, it will give an adverse taste of the alcohol, as well as the scent of it will be far too strong, giving a perception that the sake is off. If you are to warm a sake lightly, then it will offer an intense flavor, with more umami. The warm temperature will mute the aroma of the sake.

Determining the Right Temperature

If either temperature can lead to the sake being undrinkable, how can you determine the right temperature for your sake? A few rules apply to help you distinguish your sake and its taste:

Scent

Start with checking the scent of the sake. If the bottle has either a floral or fruity scent, then the sakes are best served chilled. The essence added to these sakes easily evaporates when heated for a warmer drink. Hence, you will lose the property of the sake. If a sake has a richer, earthier scent to it, then these are warmed to bring out the fragrance more of the sake.

Tone

Much like above, if a sake has an earthier or richer rice taste to it, these are to be warmed up to liven the taste of the drink. At room temperature, the properties of such a sake get muted. Hence, they are warmed to rejuvenate the taste of sake. Such tones are known as the umami flavors in Japan. Do not overheat the sake. Else higher temperatures will elevate the grainy taste of the drink.

Dry Sake

Dry sakes are very different, and so is their temperature. Sakes like the Cho-Karakuchi or any other dry sake with a clearer taste due to their alcohol-based flavors, if you are to heat them at a warmer temperature, their muted tones will come out better.

Now you understand how temperature affects sake, next learn the most commonly used temperatures for a different type of sake.

Unpasteurized Sake

Unpasteurized sake is also known as the Nama-zake, it is often drunk at a cold temperature to elevate its crisp and fresh taste. If it is warm, then it will lose its crisp taste. If it is too chilled, it will lose its freshness. The best temperature is 41-50°F.

Daiginjo and Ginjo Sake

These are what people commonly refer to as premium sake due to them having a more refined taste. As a result, Junmai Daiginjo and Ginjo Sakes do not require heating to mute any off-taste or strong taste. Daiginjo sakes have ester in them that contribute to their fragrance and are heat-sensitive. If they are heated, then the heat will evaporate the ester. Thus, these are enjoyed chill. If you are to cool them a little too much, then it will start to freeze the ester and offer a bland taste instead. The best temperature for these is 50-59°F.

Junmai, Honjozo, and Futsushu

These types of sakes are most receptive to heat. Often the warming of these sakes does justice to the flavors. When heated for longer, these sakes' rich, earthy, and grainy flavors start to dull. When heated, the particles are, in a way, rejuvenated, hence enhancing the aroma and taste both. If heated too much, then the alcoholic nature of it will be stirred a little too much, giving a stronger acidic feel. The best temperature is 55-140°F.

The different types of sakes have unique properties and taste. So, surely the rules mentioned above vary. If you feel conflicted and unsure, whether you should heat your sake or not, adapt to its taste at room temperature. This is when the sake is at its optimum, and the flavors would be balanced for your palates to adjust to.

Likewise, if you are feeling adventurous, you can attempt to heat your sake. Nonetheless, you cannot pour the liquid in a microwave or over a saucepan on high flame. There is a specific method to heat your sake if you do not wish to corrode the sake.

The ideal way of heating sake is to stir its contents subtly and give a good boost to the flavors that have been at rest for some time. Avoid direct heat to not destroy the alcohol or ester in the sake. Thus, it is best to prepare a water bath. Heat half a pan of the saucepan on the stove. Once you feel the water is warm (do not boil the water), take it off the stove and place the saucepan on a countertop. Gently, submerge your bottle of sake in it. Ensure that the level of water is never above the level of sake. Let your bottle dip in for 10 minutes maximum before you serve it.

The method of dipping sake in hot water is for when you have to heat your sake. More restaurants are now adopting this method as well as serving sake in the traditional Japanese way. Yet, there is a particular way to serve sake. From the terminologies of when ordering different sakes, at a different temperature, to the entire etiquette of serving sake, we know sake is not only a beverage, but also a culture that one experiences. If you wish to step up your sake game and familiarize yourself with some of the terminologies of sake serving temperature, then the list below is just for you.

Sake Serving Temperatures

For all the sake fanatics out there, they all like their sake at a certain temperature. To aid such people, the Japanese have coined different terms for sake at different temperatures for people when they would place their orders. Of course, each temperature offers a different burst of flavor. Let's understand them.

Tobikirikan: 131°F

Tobikirikan (extremely hot) is flaming hot, offering an intense flavor. Only heat enough sake to drink at once. The temperature of sake can roughly be measured by the temperature of the water used to heat the tokkuri.

Atsukan: 122°F

While the temperature is not as hot as Tobikirikan, Atsukan (very hot) still brings out a strong taste, with an equally dry texture of the drink.

Jokan: 113°F

Most people love Jokan (slightly hot) for its smoke-breathing liquid when poured in a glass. It gives the effect of a dragon blaze, as the flavor, too, is sharp and warm.

Nurukan: 104°F

Nurukan (gently warmed) is the closest to the body temperature, letting the liquid still be warm. The result offers a very fragrant sake to be enjoyed.

Hitohadakan: 95°F

Hitohadakan (body temperature) temperature falls a little lower than our body temperature, so the liquid is still warm but not quite as much. At this temperature, you can get a good whiff of the grainy nature of the sake.

Hinatakan: 86°F

Hinatakan (sunbathing warmth) falls perfectly between our body temperature and room temperature. At this, we get to enjoy a velvety texture of the sake, with the fragrances enhanced.

Hiya: 64 – 82°F

Hiya (not warmed) refers to the room temperature at which we purchase our sake. Hiya is a popular temperature with sake enthusiasts nowadays but use to be Japanese thought drinking Hiya-zake is not a healthy practice.

Suzuhie: 59°F

Suzuhie (lightly chilled) falls a little below the room temperature, thickening the texture of the sake and a rich aroma.

Hanahie: 50°F

Hanahie (chilled flower) is achieved when you place your sake in the fridge for a couple of hours. The result is usually a clearer taste of the sake. The aroma starts to dull at this temperature.

Yukihie: 41°F

If you have placed your sake in the fridge and forgotten all about it for more than a couple of hours, chances are your bottle is now at Yukihie (snow chilled) temperature where both the flavor and scent of the drinks are dull but the taste is clean.

Concept of Receptacle Usage

There are tea ceremonies in Japan that were originally started by Sen no Rikyū from Osaka. In 1579, Rikyū became a tea master for Oda Nobunaga. Following Nobunaga's death in 1582, he was a tea master for Toyotomi Hideyoshi. Hideyoshi had moved the capital of Japan to Osaka and built tea houses in Fushimi. Rikyū then hosted tea ceremonies to entertain politically important figures.

Such ceremonies are hosted where tea is steeped and brewed in tearooms, portraying art and history. It is nearly the same for sake. There are etiquettes to drinking sake, which most people might not know living abroad. Sake can be simply clinked and drunk, or received in a sake receptacle.

There are special customary ways of drinking sake when in social gatherings. To begin with, one cannot pour their own sake, it is poured by the host. The drinker is to cup the holder with one hand and place the other hand beneath the holder to support, while the host is to fill the holder of sake. Usually, the younger ones in the gathering are to pour the drink as a means of showing respect for the elders present. Likewise, when pouring, the host is to hold the sake with both hands. I know you must be eager to drink your sake by now, but in Japan, it is leisurely enjoyed. So when your host has poured you a serving, you are to take a sip before resting the cup on the table.

The reason behind such a way of serving is the originating of sake. It was drunk when commemorating occasions or religious rituals. Thus, even the way of serving was full of respect and etiquette, one which is still adapted when people celebrate in Japan. Sakes are commonly poured from a vessel called Tokkuri carafe, whereas the types of cups or glasses for drinking are various, but Ochoko is commonly used.

The receptacles for drinking are various, and the ones used in such occasions consist of an Ochuko, Masu, or Sakazuki. A Sakazuki is a saucer-like drinking bowl used during ceremonies. A Masu, the original and traditional receptacle, is a wooden, box-like cup. It was used as a rice-measuring tool when farmers discovered that it could be used as a receptacle too due to its antibacterial nature. Since then, Masu cups are used to enhance the aroma of the sake due to being made from cedar-wood or Hinoki. During ceremonies, the hosts construct a pyramid out of the Masu. The number of Masus used is to represent the number of guests they have and are stacked over one another. It is a moment full of wonderment as the host carefully pours a bottle of sake in the Masu at the top of the pyramid and continues to pour until all the contents of the bottle overflow and fill the other Masu beneath. The momentum depicts the motion of a waterfall.

What I love the most about this is the reason behind this simple gesture of gratitude of the host for their guests. The overflowing of sake to fill the cups below is to portray that the host is sharing their bounty, generosity, and kindness with their guests, celebrating the happiness of the host. In turn, the host shows how they are sharing their joy and well-wishes with all those who come in the motion of the sake being shared from the top glass, with those supporting it.

Let's take a moment to digest all this information. It is no shock that sake is not only a beverage, but also symbolizes joy and celebration. Now comes the next big question we keep coming across – what food is best enjoyed with sake?

Sake Food Pairing

Like every other aspect, this part of the sake journey is just as intriguing. While sake accompanies meals well, certain types of sakes bring out the most flavor in a certain food. Unlike wine, sake can bring out the flavor in a wide range of meals. Some of the sakes bring out the most. The three things we need to keep in mind are the following: *Flavor*, *Texture*, and *Acidity*.

Flavor

Understanding how sake has both, a denser flavor and a lighter flavor, these can be matched with food to either complement it, or to provide a contrast by matching the opposite. For example, a dish like a light fish can be paired with a light sake to complement it or with a heavier sake to provide contrast and heighten the dining experience.

Texture

A sake can either be thick or light. Hence, the texture of sake can be mixed-and-matched with that of food as well. You can opt for a light sake with a pickled vegetable for contrast, or match it with ramen to complement your meal. You can also choose a thicker sake for roasted meat-based meals, or a lighter one to gulp down the meaty feast.

Acidity

This is an important factor to consider when it comes to pairing food with sake. There is acid in your sake. So, if a sake has a higher acidic content, and so does your meal.

Similarly, if you pair an acidic sake with a meal lighter in acidic nature, sake can bring out the flavors in the meal.

Pair a dry Junmai with a meal, rich in fats and meat so that it can help burst the juices in your meal.. Likewise, you can pair a Junmai, high in alcohol content, with sushi, and it will bring out the flavors of sushi the most. If your Junmai has a good level of acid, then you can pair it with a salad to elevate the flavors of the vegetables.

For a Honjozo, the sake has a stronger flavor, packed with punches of alcohol, and hence can be enjoyed with simpler meals, like Ramen. For a Daiginjo, we know that the unpasteurized liquid offers an earthy taste, hence we can pair it with mushrooms or even tempura to enhance their strong flavors.

Now that you know which type of sake is best enjoyed at which temperature and with which food, I am certain that you can dazzle your guest the next time you head out for an all-Japanese cuisine experience.

Chapter 9
Health Benefits of Sake

Is sake good for health?

Koji is certified as a "national mold" in Japan as it has been used in various foods and contributed to rich food culture. Koji has various health benefits, and so does sake that is fermented with Koji and yeast. It is truly a bottle of wonderment, wholesome nectar full of goodness. Not many people are aware of sake's offerings. Most patrons that show up at the tasting room do so based on word-of-mouth advertising.

Some patrons have shared how they come to know of the tasting room – it is through Yelp after they Google. It is shocking for me to learn that 60% of them have never even heard of sake, let alone taste it. 30% of them have never consumed alcohol. So, why are people driven to the sake tasting room when a part of them do not even consume alcohol? I believe that it is the very thought of a person trying sake for the first time from a cup is very intriguing. When I served sake to the patrons in BRC, it felt as if I was pouring them a cup of enchanted liquid that would bewitch them. There, I came across a blonde guy, Phi. He shared how he had driven all the way from Arizona alone. To me, he sounded like a school teacher, but he was a self-declared inventor that was among the people who stayed at the

Burning Man event until the final day.

"You know, I used to work for a pharmaceutical distribution company. They were playing a substantial role in the opioid epidemic. My experience over there left me with one mystery, why are normal folks living in suburban midwest addicted to an irreversible health risk?" I do not know what led me to direct this question at Phi, but his answer was one that brought insight.

"I think they are doing meaningless stuff on a daily basis, hoping to find an underlying meaning within them."

Phi's reply was the same answer that Eizo, the sushi chef, gave me. I was taken aback. On the third day of the Burning Man Event, Eizo had served his last sushi before asking David and me to join him for supper – the retrospective meeting. Instead, Eizo spent the time chatting away. He shared how he was born and brought up in Nagano. Nagano had been the destination for the Winter Olympics.

"Wow," I said, "That's amazing. You can ski and or snowboard every winter then?" "You know, you should do meaningful things in life, and then skiing is fun, but sadly I didn't do it. I missed the opportunity. I spent my time smoking pot. Thankfully, I managed to escape the clutches of those horrid times, and now, I think I should open my own restaurant in San Jose."

My point of sharing the above information is to highlight an overview of life. A soul tends to find ways to search for the unhealthy source of happiness for mental health, which takes a toll on physical health in the end. I admit that I, too, at times, rely on alcohol to release my stress. But I drink just as much as it is needed to fill me with a sense of comfort temporarily.

It is stressful to be living and working in San Francisco but then like most Americans, I have a day job that prohibits me from being addicted to alcohol or any form of prescribed or illegal drugs. In a nutshell, I am unable to drink hard liquor since they remain in my body for a prolonged period of time. Hence, my preference shifts to either wine or beer. Even then, I have to cut down more on wine as it is acidic and hurts my stomach. I tend to get an allergic reaction when I drink wine. I guess it has to do with the sulfite in the wine, and that my stomach cannot tolerate more than a certain amount of it. If you are to search for this, you will come to know that wine contains about 5mg to 200mg of sulfite per liter. In case you are unaware, the legal consumption limit in the United States is 350 mg per liter. Due to this, most people usually order dry wine, as a standard bottle of dry red wine contains about 50 milligrams in a liter. For this reason, I had to switch from wine to sake, apart from sake being readily accessible from work, aka the sake tasting room.

The patrons that stumbled into the tasting room shared a similar story with me. They came to the tasting room alone over the weekend as it made them feel a lot happier, and their happiness would last until the end of the day. I found this to be true because I could see their faces light up once they finished their tasting course. Call it magic or science, whatever the reason, I saw it be true that sake truly had benefits.

What are the Health Benefits of Sake?

For long, we have linked wine with relaxation. It is our comfort zone, and when we seek the kind of comfort we want, our eyes only wander as far as the wine aisle. If you have a hectic and sweaty routine after yoga, if your Yin class is not relaxing enough, if you are looking for a way to balance out your relaxation post-workout, or if you wish to blow off some steam without breaking out in sweats, perhaps you will reach out your arm to grasp a bottle of wine. But have you ever thought of sake instead of wine? What if I tell you that a glass of sake may offer you more than just relaxation? We already know that sake is brewed differently than other alcoholic beverages, which is one of the reasons that already sets the drink apart from its counterparts.

When I first got a job at the sake tasting room, during

training I was told their parent brewery in Kyoto is doing very well financially because of their biotechnology subsidiary. They studied Koji and discovered an anticancer agent in Koji enzymes in 1967. Moreover, on March 5, 2020 their bioventures announced that it will work with Osaka University to develop a DNA vaccine to prevent the transmission of the new coronavirus. It is very exciting that they can end a pandemic crisis, but excess consumption of sake can pose a threat to the liver like any other alcoholic beverage. After all, alcohol takes a longer time to be either absorbed in or excreted from our system. Only when sake is consumed in a limit, the Koji and amino acids can do the exact opposite.

High in nutrients

This sounds a little too good to be true, doesn't it? However, it is every bit true. Given that sake is fermented, it allows for the drink to develop on its own while producing nutrients during the process. So each time you are sipping on sake, you are sipping Vitamin A, Vitamin B1, and Vitamin B6.

Low in calories

I cannot resist reiterating this point. Since most of the starch and sugar is converted, there is a smaller amount of sugar present in sake, hence giving it a lower calorie count. So, you can sip on sake without guilt now.

Obesity who?

Granted, there are fewer calories in sake. Apart from that, sake is known for entailing good starch-absorbing abilities and boosting proteins. The absence of carbohydrates and sugar in the drink allows you to place a glass of sake on your dining mat, even when you are dieting.

Good bacteria

Remember how Koji is sprinkled on the rice grains throughout the brewing of sake? Well, they not only aid in the conversion of starch but are also good bacteria that boost your immune system.

Probiotic goodness

After undergoing fermentation, the drink also produces lactic acid. We know that lactic acid bacteria are probiotics. What do probiotics do? They aid in restoring our intestinal health while also improving our digestive system.

A stable digestive system

Do probiotics present in sake alone offer good digestive health? No. Although sake contains a fair amount of citric acid and lactic acid, they help elevate the digestion process by breaking down food quicker, hence improving the overall health of our stomach.

Diabetes prevention – a myth?

People often put forth an argument of sake, helping with preventing diabetes. While sake does not prevent diabetes drastically, it does play a role in doing so. The low content of sugar makes sake a safe drink, even for diabetic patients. But they should consume it in a limited amount. Certain sakes are known as carriers of an insulin-sort of catalyst. As of now, such a catalyst is found in Namazake Sake.

Lesser risk of osteoporosis

Most of the sugary drinks out there pose a threat to our bones. They can corrode the calcium present in our body, weakening them and making us more prone to osteoporosis. Sake, on the other hand, is different. The amino acids present in it are the restorers and guardians of bones. Koji is one of the defenders of bones as well. Koji is known for containing a certain assortment of Cathepsin-L, an enzyme catalyst that can help with the prevention of osteoporosis.

Low blood pressure

Sake has three peptides that prevent heart diseases such as angina, stroke, and heart attack.

Better blood circulation

These peptides have enzymes that help stabilize your blood flow by preventing clots. If you are suffering from a cold or frozen shoulder, sake can help you by easing the clots.

Regulated cholesterol level

Given how sake helps with easing the blood flow, it goes on to further prevent blood from clotting and cholesterol from being deposited in our arteries. The enzymes present in sake simply prevent cholesterol deposits in our body. Furthermore, sake is a good booster of high-density lipoproteins in the blood that are known for preventing cardiovascular diseases.

Less cancer risk

Remember the amino acids present in sake? These amino acids are known for combatting, shriveling, and eradicating cancer-causing substances from our bodies. Sake hinders the growth of cancerous cells in the bladder, uterine, and prostate. It also lowers the risk of cirrhosis and lung cancer.

That is not all. Apart from the amino acid, sake contains glucosamine as well. For those of you who do not know, glucosamine is a compound commonly found in the fluids around joints. It aids in the development of cartilage and much more. More importantly, glucosamine regenerates an anti-tumor catalyst that kills cancer cells.

Reduction in ulcers and gastritis

All the acids and enzymes present in sake work well together to ensure that you do not suffer from indigestion or any other digestive disorder if you drink too much sake. The enzymes work as a catalyst to break down all that you consume while boosting your immune system and reducing the production of ulcers or gastritis. But always remember to drink sake in a limited proportion, as excess is not good. It can give off an acidic burn in your stomach.

Offers selenium

Sake offers an abundance of Selenium. Selenium is a form of nutrient that helps avoid the production of bad bacteria and the contraction of viruses while elevating your metabolism as well. If you are to drink sake with a dish that is a good source of Selenium, it will only offer you a greater advantage. So, do remember to pair your sake with a good plate of tuna or sushi next time.

Avoids free radicals

Given the Selenium present in sake, the nutrient doubles up to act as an antioxidant as well. To know that it contains antioxidants is already a treat. It helps avoid free radicals present in the shape of pollutants, unhealthy fats, alcohol, and so on. Free radicals damage our cells, while the antioxidants combat the damage our cell membranes, DNA structure, and proteins incur.

Better skin

Sake is rich in antioxidants. The antioxidants promote better elasticity of the skin by stimulating the skin's sensory neurons. With better elasticity, the texture of our skin improves, giving us a more youthful look. We have heard how Japanese integrate rice in their skin, some even using rice water as toners. The reason behind this is simple – it is because of the presence of saccharides and amino acids. They help restore moisture within the epidermal layer of our skin, offering a good glow and dewy skin.

Sake, a whitener

Rice grains can whiten the skin. While this statement is partially untrue, it is partially true as well. See, you cannot alter your natural skin color, but over time when exposed to pollution and UV rays, our skin gets damaged. Koji and other substances present in sake can be the obstacle in the production of melanin - the culprit that harms and discolors the skin. These substances remove the tan from our skin. The antioxidants work to rebuild the skin layer, thus bringing forth a clear and glowing complexion.

A great moisturizer

Not that one needs a reason to try sake, but if the above-mentioned benefits have failed to fascinate you, then this reason can be another one to intrigue you. Dry skin is a nightmare. It leaves your skin parched, forming dark spots that scream for you to hydrate it. Then comes the second part, either you let your skin be, which will leave you with the urge to scratch, or you opt for a moisturizer.

Even then, moisturizers provide a temporary effect. What if you drink a liquid that can fight signs of dry skin? Sake contains an array of nutrients that rebuild your skin. The amino acids, vitamins, and saccharides breathe life into damaged skin layers, reviving the shriveling cells. In fact, rice has been used as a treatment by the Japanese for so many years. Cosmetic giants having conducted research were bewildered to discover that most rice farmers or people working with rice had youthful skin. The reason was that the rice grain contains enough nutrients to promote better and hydrated skin. All of such are steeped in greater volumes when sake is brewed.

By learning about sake in detail and sharing all the information with you, I aim to project more reasons for people to try out sake. Wine, too, has many benefits, but it is heavy for the body. Sake, in such a scenario, turns out to be an exemplary alternative. So, while you are sipping on your glass of sake leisurely, you will be offering your body the nutrients that will be improving your overall health. I hope these reasons are enough for you to keep a bottle of sake in your liquor cabinet, at least.

Chapter 10
Sake Breweries around the World

Can you find breweries in your city?

Piping hot sake in sushi bars has been around for more than forty years in American metropolitan cities. Most of the patrons present at a sake tasting room have confessed to having initially tried the drink at a sushi restaurant. This lead me to assume that the restaurant must be generating its revenue margin more from a fixed price of fish and a lower cost of sake, which is kept steady.

One thing these restaurants failed to take care of was the condition of keeping a sake bottle. See, a sake bottle is to be kept away from direct sunlight, in a cool and dry place. Any given bottle can only last you a good six months, granted it is refrigerated. Even if not opened, the shelf life of sake is one year. This stresses the need to heat sake before being served. The purpose is to kill the germs since most of these restaurants fail to maintain proper care of the bottle. At least this used to be the case ten years ago. The situation is far different now. About 18,651 restaurants have opened up, generating a revenue of $22 billion in 2019 alone. These restaurants no longer restrict their selection of servings, from hot-table sake to premium Ginjo, Daiginjo, and Tokubetsu Junmai, which are all served chilled.

What surprises me is that high-end chilled sakes are not

only served at Michelin starred sushi bars, Asian eateries, but also at French restaurants. The French chef and sommelier, Beige Alan Ducasse, brews sake himself to serve at his restaurant. The era of Japanese sake being made by French in Paris has come. There is another French man Nicolas Jules who works on it. His sake is named "AYAM", and is brewed at his gin distillery in Paris, "Distillery de Paris". He uses short grain table rice and red rice from Camargue, France, which is a famous rice production area in France. The Koji he uses is a hybrid koji made from a mixture of koji brought back from Japan and koji used in Chinese yellow sake. The use of two types of rice, the use of hybrid koji, and the unfiltered bottling are to enhance the taste of the ingredients to achieve the very original flavor. It was sake, which was dry and had a strong koji flavor. Both French sakes are served chilled.

When I was serving at the BRC, I never served hot sake. This amazed some of the most affluent burners. They would simply say, "Wow, this is amazing. I never had anything like this before."

It was the different texture brought to us, leading to patrons having requested to refill their cups again and again and again. You see, the essence of a good sake is its freshness, especially if served chill. If this is the case, then where do these restaurants get their share of sake from?

Over the years, as Japanese culture gained popularity, so did the food. Who doesn't appreciate the melt-in-your-mouth texture of wagyu beef or the exquisite and tantalizing taste of Bluefin tuna sushi? Let's not forget the pocket-friendly ramen quickly gaining fame among dorm students at the end of the month. Surely, Japanese food sprawled over the world within a short amount of time. Sake is now widely available, from five-star restaurants to neighborhood shops. Even variations of sake are available at local markets around the globe.

It seems people around the globe are craving for more and more of the Japanese cuisine. This is why it does not surprise me that the growth in sake sales has escalated as well. From my time at the tasting room to the BRC, this is one thing I witnessed firsthand. People were amazed each time I served them a sake cocktail. Nonetheless, as the demand prospered, it blossomed an opportunity - an opportunity for sommeliers and sake fanatics to expand their expertise. Today, breweries are standing tall and functioning seamlessly to meet the ever-growing demands of the consumers everywhere.

Breweries opened one after another, even if some had drastically closed off in Japan. The international fame of sake resurrected its dying fandom back in Japan. I am sure if you are to look for the statistics on this, you can easily come across an array of links on search engines that will give you an outlook on just how sales doubled over the past decade.

Are people craving for a change?

As a consumer, my demand for something new, something different, surely puts a business in a more competitive state. Companies have to develop newer and unique formulas to make their products distinct from their competitors.

Now sommeliers and breweries are coming out of their comfort zones to cope with new trends. Sake around the world is creating an experience. The drink is no longer focused on refined elements. Instead, sake is revamping itself to be a drink that will linger a little longer on your taste buds, a drink that will offer you the promise of happiness, with hints of confidence and comfort. It is still a celebratory beverage but not confined to it. In the San Francisco Bay Area alone, there are two sake microbreweries – Squire Sake and Den Sake.

They brew with the availability of Calrose rice cultivated in Sacramento Valley. The rice grain falls between short to medium length. As for the water, it is supplied from the snow-melted water from the Sierra Nevada. These are not the only ones, but there are also Japanese establishments having ventured overseas after four decades of survival.

Sake sommeliers have moved toward craft sake. One such example is none other than Takagi Akitsuna, the fifteenth generation of Takagi Shuzo.

For those who are unaware, Takagi took over a 400-year-old Yamagata District brewery at a young age of 21. The man is a genius. He is a maestro who swore to alter the fate of sake. He is the man behind Juyondai – a drink having gained all eyes from the cosmopolitan region, the villages in Japan, and in the western world. Everyone only had to take one sip of it before they would be left craving for more. Juyondai created an unquenchable thirst, lifting its demand.

What Takagi did was give a flickering ray of hope for sake and a reason for it to strive. He showed to the world that sake has so much more to offer. That it is a life that only needed a pair of hands to mold and shapes it. From one end of the world to the other, breweries across the world have not only perfected the origins but also dared to meddle with the sacred taste, to birth a different shade of sake in the hopes of matching limitless moods of their consumers. Umami Insider magazine concludes that in spite of sake being around for eons, its concept is still new-found in America.

It does not matter if you are sipping on it in California or experiencing it in a tasting room in New York, you will be offered a vast spectrum of traditional as well as craft sakes in the U.S. Do you want to catch a quick glimpse at some of the now prestigious and renowned breweries around the world? Let's have a look.

Zenkuro – New Zealand

Based in Queenstown, sake has cast a spell on New Zealanders to the point that they opened their own brewery named Zenkuro. It is New Zealand's first and only brewery to date. From Junmai to Ginjo, they brew a blend of sake that is as unique as creating a kiwi flavor. This is how they devised their names as well. Zen translates into entirely, and Kuro translates into the black – a blend that depicts strength and power. New Zealand is all about that.

They tend to polish their rice to about 60%, bringing out the maximum starch content present in the rice grain. This offers its consumers the 'premium taste'. While sake tends to come at 18% of alcohol, Zenkuro uses New Zealand's optimum water to lower the percentage, bringing it to 14.5%.

Kanpai London Craft Sake – U.K.

Soaking in inspiration from a day spent at a bar tucked in Kyoto, the creators behind London Craft sake returned home to share their experience with the rest of Peckham, London. They found sake to be a drink more than just a warm alcoholic beverage served with a piping hot bowl of noodles. They stumbled upon what sake truly was – a drink as unique as Japanese culture. From being self-taught to refining their skills at breweries in Japan, Kanpai London brought their talent to start as home-based craftsmanship.

It was only a matter of time before their interest in the refined drink spread throughout the U.K. Their passion was indefinite. They did not only want to recreate the Japanese way of brewing sake, but they also wanted to go beyond their horizon to offer a different experience altogether. They started to experiment with various styles by using different ratios of ingredients, adding additional flavors, and altering yeasts. Their goal remains to serve fresh sake each time.

Keeping the goal in mind, Lucy Holmes and Tom Wilson, the husband and wife behind Kanpai London, brew their sake in their spare room within the vicinity of their London flat. Still, they managed to brew their third batch, selling their drinks at renowned departmental stores such as Selfridge. Their drinks may be limited in number, but they have experimented with clear Junmai-style sake and cloudy Nigori sake.

Sake One – U.S.

America's very first sake brewery, Sake One, is based in Oregon. From the waters of Oregon's valley, they brew award-winning sakes such as the Momokawa, Moonstone, and Yomi. Working under the supervision of Toji, Sake One now offers more premium sake, some of which are craft-brewed lines supported by international brands Kasumi Tsuru, Yoshinogawa, Murai Family, Hakutsu, Sake Moto, Kibo, and Tombo. Their sake is crafted from local ingredients. It is no wonder that they have acquired more awards than any other brewery in America, and surely their sake must be worth the shot.

Go Shu Sake – Australia

Standing gracefully amongst the Blue Mountains, Go Shu Sake brewery is amongst the leading sake breweries in Australia. What makes it unique is their state-of-the-art facility brewery, where the magic takes place. This magic is visible to visitors who can opt to take a tour of the facility. Go Shu Sake brewers aim to create awareness among Australian folks about what sake truly is. Their premium sake enchants each person who leaves the facility. Go Shu focuses on the alternatives of Premium sake out there. From light floral notes to dry, full-bodied, fruity, bitter, and lighter sakes, their range is extensive, just as their goals are.

Nogne O – Norway

Nogne O Det Kompromisslose Brygeri, or known as The Uncompromising Brewery in English, is a Norway-based, Striving to brew sake with utmost honesty and integrity,

Nogne O grips tightly to the olden means of the brewery. Each sake they brew is Yamahai, and only Ginpu rice imported from Hokkaido is used. Nogne O is also dedicated to crafting sake from Yamahai Moto and other naturally produced yeasts.

Nogne O is the artist behind their famous Nogne O beers. Keeping their virtues in mind, they proceeded to venture toward sake brewing as well. After much thought, they made their logo, which characters read Hadaka Jima Nogne O. The translation is equally fascinating, Naked Island from Norwegian. Due to their labor-intensive craftsmanship, the company makes an equally power-packed sake with a bold and complex taste that is a crowd-pleaser. All of this, they owe to the dedication of their master brewers, labor, and distinctive ingredients imported straight from Japan. Nogne O sure knows how to bring the best of both worlds for consumers in Europe.

Artisan Sake Maker – Canada

Based in Granville Island, Canada, Artisan Sake produces a line of sake by the name of Osake, winning awards and the hearts of many in Canada and around the world. What makes their premium sake so unique? It is the care and devotion of the workers. It is them brewing sake in smaller batches while looking into the procedure closely to ensure quality. They believe in growing their own products that will be used during the brewing process. They do not just stop there but go beyond to use the leftover rice in other cuisines.

Their Junmai is hand-pressed, hand-bottled, unfiltered, and unpasteurized to offer the consumers with the freshest taste sake could possibly have. In the hopes of meeting consumer demand, while sake is produced once a year in Japan during winters, Artisan Sake makers brew throughout the year in smaller cycles. Of course, this requires them to adapt, change, and improvise their strategies without compromising their principles. What better than to taste fresh Junmai that is unique to each season and that complements the meals of those particular seasons well? I surely understand why Canadians are so fond of their Osake.

Takara Sake USA – Berkeley, CA

Located in sunny Berkeley, California, Takara Sake USA. features a tasting room, and a museum, to provide consumers with the best time while being there. Its tasting room features a fusion of traditional and the Berkeley original sake.

Gekkeikan Sake (USA)

Gekkeikan sake was the first to inaugurate a brewery in Folsom, California, in 1989. Its tasting room is as unique as its sake. With a Japanese garden and koi pond as part of the room, you will relax within the Zen-like aura.

Brewers that aided in globalizing sake

Decades ago, the world was in the dark about Japanese culture. Even if it was talked about, no one truly knew the depths of what Japanese cuisine was like, until tourists and locals embarked on a journey with the sole mission to expand. Later bringing a piece of Japan to showcase to the rest of the world. Most of these companies had been local, providing sake with the rightful limelight of innovation and marketing as they extended their products overseas. Let's take a glimpse at some of them.

Dassai

Sake rose and then faded in Japan. Thousands of breweries were put out of business. Like a rapid wildfire, the blazes of sake devotion died too. Still, some companies stood tall through the harshest storm of decline. One such company is Asahi Shuzo. The company was close to filing for bankruptcy until Sakurai took over the business from his father, saving it from a devastating fate and giving the company a brand new life.

The company devised premium Junmai sake in the hopes

of reviving its tarnishing repute, and before the company knew it, its innovation was a fan-favorite. Within a couple of years, its Junmai became its prestigious asset. After the introduction of Dassai, people were quick to turn their heads in the direction of the premium sake. Bit by bit, Dassai became a delicacy for social events and celebrations across the world.

Juyondai

If you have ever visited a liquor store in Japan, you may see a particular sake brand chained to the shelves. You may wonder, "Why this particular sake chained when there are more expensive bottles available?" The truth is, this particular sake, Juyondai, is the most-sought cult brand and worth committing a crime for it. The creators of Juyondai, which means the fourteenth generation, put his minds together, playing with flavors that were beyond delicate.

What made the bold and majestic sake mysteriously unique was the fact that it came only once in a quarter. Even then, the bottles were limited, causing its price to hike. Sake enthusiasts were willing to pay whatever the price, for they deemed it to be the crown among their collection.

Kubota

In theory, premium sake is clean, yet full-bodied, well-balanced, and well-distinct. Kubota Daiginjo well-defies this concept not just in theory. All these separate elements, although hard to find them all in one bottle, they all came to life in the form of Kubota. Soon enough, Kubota started making rounds beyond its neighboring vicinity, with fruity and velvety tones. It was a dance of honeysuckle and tuberose, a fusion of Fuji apples and pears, all the while offering a kick of sake that flowed seamlessly together.

Kubota, in itself, is a wonderment, from it's bursting taste to evened flavors, Kubota is a fine craft that managed to regain its reign. It inspires others to follow in its footsteps of fruity sake, with flavors that blend well.

Hakkaisan

With the idea of offering a rich drink that is clean, flavorful on its own, and does not interfere with other tastes when paired with a meal, Tojis over at Hakkaisan managed to manifest into their vision. By directing an abundance of the freshest of spring waters from Hakkaisan (Mt. Hakkai) straight to their brewery, the water is one of their weapons used in the creation of Hakkaisan Sake. Their end-to-end process is precautions maintained at all times. They offer a delicate table sake loved by all.

What sets Hakkaisan apart, on top of the fact that they can deliver sake around the world? Well, it is their ability and devotion to meet the unquenchable thirst of the market by producing throughout the season. In times when breweries only brew once and then take a break until next season, Hakkaisan does the exact opposite. Their continuous production without compromising the drink's quality, as they only add a measured amount of ingredients for one batch, Hakkaisan has been a promise never to be broken to its admirers.

Kokuryu

In a market brimming with innovation, where brewers were working relentlessly to offer a vast spectrum of flavors, Kokuryu uniquely innovated sake. After all, they had been in the game since 1804, located in the valley of Fukui.

What was the maximum period brewers would leave their sake for maturation? One month? Five years? It is anytime from two to four months. While Kokuryu had already meddled with the flavors, they brought about Daiginjo that was light, dense, complex, clean, fruity, and floral. They became the first to incorporate the French wine maturation technique. Not only was the company cultivating its own ingredients and using the freshest source of water, but they also varied the maturation technique for sake, giving it a remodeled taste. As always, Kokuryu managed to impress their clientele once again with their latest technique, and gained attention from markets and sommeliers around the world.

Sudo Honke

Sudo Honke was established in 1141. The brewery is located in an area called Obara, in Ibaraki state originally. The history they have is a bit different from other breweries; the family started as samurai with a mission of revitalizing the economy and with the goal, they started brewing sake.

Sudo Honke has managed to stand strong and garner fame from around the world. The 55th generation of the samurai family now runs it. Samurais know how to fight and how to survive, and this helped the family persevere in their mission. The family fought day and night against all the odds, and it led their heritage to continue to thrive. It was only in 1995 when they first exported sake to the U.S. and then to France. From there, their business only continued to climb a greater level of success.

Takara

Much like Sudo Honke, Takara sake was brewed by the Takara group after the Edo period in 1842. Over the next two decades, they were able to venture toward brewing Shochu, Mirin, and Shirozake. Takara did not stop its journey there. Takara went after the market trends from its decline in sales to the rising demands for its distinct sake.

It was the struggle and efforts of Usaburo Yomo and Kurakichi Ohmiya, both of whom worked together to not only enhance their sales, but to also acquire more companies. Even after the effects of WWII, Takara managed to secure sales by solely relying on Shochu, which contributed to 28% of its sales. By 1951, it was exporting products to the U.S., starting from California. Over the next ten years, Takara was found being served in many Japanese restaurants in the U.S.

Gekkeikan

Gekkeikan Junmai sake happens to be a cult-favorite for good reasons. From their 370-year-old journey, their unique Junmai style offers herb-influenced fruity notes, with underlying tones of earthiness. They are truly a wizard of flavors. Gekkeikan understands the process, technique, and flavors of sake in such depth that it can bring out the best in each kind.

Companies tend to limit their flavor range and experiment with them. But if you are to look for a Gekkeikan, you will come across brews that are acidic yet humble, exotic yet familiar, and complex yet clean. One of the many reasons why people love Gekkeikan is that it is not limited to a serving style or temperature. You can enjoy it hot with your sushi or cold with steak. The choice is yours.

Ozeki Sake

Ozeki was quick to acquire the attention and favorability of Americans. It is the warmth of it and its freshness as they sip it gingerly. It is that go-to clean, smooth, and rich sake, best enjoyed warm by Americans when sake was first introduced in the States. To date, it still remains a popular choice. They managed to open the brewery in 1979 in Hollister, California. A location where they had access to local ingredients such as Calrose rice and water from the Sierra Nevada and used them in such harmony to produce a hyper-local sake, capturing the true essence of Northern California.

Yaegaki

This is another drink natives and non-natives adore due to its food-friendly nature. It does not upset your stomach while providing you with a dry, wine-like, and crisp taste. What amazes patrons is that Yaegaki goes with anything and everything; It is an affable drink. With a history that expands over more than 350 years, Yaegaki was quick to jump on the modernized wagon of brewing as it realized the hike in demand and uses present-day biotechnology. Yaegaki started producing sake in the U.S. in 1987.

Otokoyama

This sake originated from the Edo period, and it was just as popular then as it is today. From taking great precautions and paying attention to each procedure during the brewing process, Otokoyama was able to offer a dry yet refreshing sake to the consumers in Japan. With time, they realized the importance of bringing its product to a bigger market and began to exhibit their product in 1977 at the Monde Selection.

From there, the brewers continued to promote their sake and brought bottles after bottles to each exhibition they heard of. Their efforts finally paid off in 1984 when their Otokoyama sake won a gold medal, and began exporting sake to the U.S. As of today, Otokoyama exports to over twenty countries, and their breweries have been converted into museums for customers to witness their process firsthand.

Setting Sun Sake Brewing Company

If you want to find yourself a bottle of craft sake in San Diego, Setting Sun Sake Brewing Company is undoubtedly the place to go. With locally produced ingredients and a mission to bring about the future of sake in the United States, this brewery has a tasting room. The visitors can sample their creative brews. Setting Sun has a unique approach to sake, even offering sake that has been dry-hopped like beer. Enjoy an indeed artisan sake with original taste.

Sequoia Sake

If you are on the hunt to find the freshest sake in San Francisco, then head over to Sequoia Sake. It is a brewery that is as fascinating and natural as the West Coast. Their aim is to extend its brews to the mass population and show off its artistry through versatile drinks that can be paired with just about anything. While only offering Junmai-style sake, their simple recipe is worthy of applause. The richness and intricate details of its brew are available for touring and private events at their tasting room, which keeps consumers hooked.

Texas Sake Company

While it has moved away from the West Coast and moved down South, its small-batched based brews are still true to their original recipe. Texas Sake is pioneering a new palette in America.

If you are intrigued by the ancient recipe it uses, then you can pay a visit to its family-friendly tasting room and try a blend of unique cocktails that they offer.

Ben's Tune-up

Ben's Tune-Up promises an American craft-beer like experience to its sake brewing. Suffice to say, the spot brings the best of both worlds, also known as beer and sake garden. Ben's Tune-up always serves its sake cold and on tap. They are making sake bar & garden a true entertainment spot when visiting the Blue Ridge Mountains. Ben's Tune-Up is located in downtown Asheville, North Carolina,

Brooklyn Kura

Kura brewery may be new to Brooklyn, but they offer a truly American experience to sake brewing. They too have taken the craft beer approach, priding itself over their manipulation of ingredients that result in a variety of sake blends. The community atmosphere of the place only elevates the Brooklyn spirit.

Blue Current Sake

This brewery brings a true coast-like experience to its sake concoctions. It uses water from Maine and rice from California to produce its award-winning Junmai and Ginjo, which are widely available across the eastern seaboard. Receiving a great amount of love from its consumers, Blue Current plans on expanding its venture to the U.K.

Den Sake Brewery

Recently established in Oakland, Den brewery is a tiny yet, brewed in small batches every 45 day all year round. They have crafted a list full of exciting restaurants in California, from Shibumi in downtown Los Angeles, Izakaya Rintaro in San Francisco, to Soba Ichi in Oakland. In February, its sake was acclaimed as a James Beard semi-finalist for wine, spirits, and beer professional awards.

Their sake is Junmai style, crafted from 70% of its original size despite the conventional preference. Based on the popular belief if a rice grain was milled more, the premium the sake was produced, but experts beg to differ now. He observed that at Soba Ichi that has a list of 10 sake bottles, out of which only one is Ginjo, and the remaining are Junmai. While Ginjo and Daiginjo can replace a cocktail, Junmai can be enjoyed instead of a glass of wine.

Den sake has more acidity like white wine than Ginjo but is yet light and has a full body to compliment local California cuisine as well as Japanese and Asian food.

Chapter 11
Sake Tasting Rooms and Tours

Do you pay for a visit to a tasting room?

In spite of tasting rooms charging a fee, people are still charmed by them. They swarm around the places that offer tasting rooms more than just taking a tour of their brewery. The tasting room offers the visitor with a piece of their history and culture. Most importantly, the brewery takes patrons through the entire process of making sake - a process of absolute enchantment. In fact, tasting rooms have become an inbound marketing aspect of tourism.

The gratitude for this notion solely goes to globalization, which brings the existence of sake breweries to a larger audience. As more and more people gain awareness, they all want to have a sip of a good liquor beverage. Hence, people would stop by these breweries to indulge in the drink and soak in the scenic atmosphere of the establishment. The trend of tourism shifted from shopping to experience. Sake breweries offer an experience.

The same was what I discovered to be true for the Burning Man Event. You see, BRC is more than just a sight of marvel. It is a metropolis, promising a united structure to be shared with a group of participants. The event gives the patrons a sense of radical self-reliance.

There seems to be a fine line between the rich and the

poor. The group of wealthy participants has a desire to adorn themselves with custom-made costumes with their own infrastructures including the solar-powered Wi-Fi system around their super lux RVs with chiefs. The purpose behind them being there is still unknown to me, but I infer these people have an urge to be provoked by something they are not easily challenged in their regular settings. The infamous story of Google hiring its CEO in BRC tells an aspect of high net worth networking.

Tasting rooms offer visitors a chance to explore how much control the brewers have and how they concoct a drink for their patron's indulgence. Visitors acquire a sense of participation and belonging to the sake community. This is the reason why there are tasting rooms around the world, to generate revenue, to market their products, to shed light on the process, and to offer the patrons a chance to be part of something more – to be part of a like-minded community.

It is true that nothing bonds people quicker than food. Food and beverages are the very core to breaking cross-cultural barriers and if an individual truly wishes to explore food and sake when visiting Japan, the ideal place for them is a tasting room.

Sake tasting vending machines in Tokyo

Sake has established its own fandom over the last forty decades outside of Japan, but not in Tokyo up until recently.

With the government's recent push to promote more rice consumption, sake related business is becoming a little more exciting than ever before.

There are so many kinds of sake available now. You can even find a wide variety of sake from the most traditional taste to an innovative brew that bespeaks the longevity of sake brands to be 500 years more in local supermarkets.

Tokyo Shoten

The name sounds odd. Can sake be bought from a vending machine? It is an innovative and convenient deal. The Tokyo Shoten Sake vending machine offers you sake at your convenience. With a wide array of sake available even from a vending machine, if you are new to the sake world, don't you worry, the machine has an option to purchase tasting cups. The idea is to aid consumers as much as sake tasting as possible. If you are someone who knows what they want, you can purchase a full bottle of your favorite sake. Unlike most Americans, some of Japanese patrons dislike the idea of talking to staff, the machine's tasting option is just perfect for them. The vending machine offers a guide in English as well, and there are various serving cups available. You can splurge without spending all your money on just one kind of sake.

Sake Shops and Bars in Tokyo

Imadeya Ginza

Now, if you are indulging in dining at the most excellent restaurants in Tokyo, know that your options go beyond the trends and eloquent cuisine. Given the ambiance of Ginza that is Tokyo's most famous upmarket shopping, dining, and entertainment district. It's featuresing numerous department stores, boutiques, art galleries, restaurants, night clubs, and cafes.

If dining is not on your to-do list, then you can simply head over to Imadeya Ginza. Imadeya Ginza was established in April 2017, located in GINZA SIX, introducing sake, shochu, and wine. Be prepared to be treated like royalty by the staff over there. Never mind the language barrier because the staff is well-versed in English, Chinese, Korean, and Spanish to be able to accommodate tourists from all over the world.

Imadeya Ginza proudly boasts an array of premium sakes. Komyo, Niizawa, and Dassai are just some of the 400 brands it offers. Furthermore, the staff is skillful in the art of understanding the depth and notes of each sake has. If you are indecisive on the taste you wish to try or entirely new to the sake world, the staff will be more than glad to offer assistance. What makes this even better is their tasting counter. You will be served up to 10 samples at a time to try and be able to find your match.

Hasegawa Saketen

If your schedule is packed while you are in Japan and are around Tokyo, then Hasegawa Saketen (Hasegawa sake shop) is the perfect place for you. While people argue there is no such thing as *perfect*, this place begs to differ. From their on-the-go sake options to selling snacks and portable sake bottle sizes, you only need to step out of your train for five minutes at the gate of Tokyo Station. Hasegawa does not offer a tasting option but occasional tasting events.

Inishie Sake

The concept of aged sake is rather ambiguous. In such a whirlwind where aged and mature sake is thought to be one, Inishie sake steps in. The motive of the store is to highlight the difference between both sakes while offering consumers with an exemplary experience. Given that the store serves aged sake, its bottles are reasonably priced and are worth every dollar you spend. The store even lets you try some of their sakes just to ensure that you do not regret your purchase.

Fujita Saketen

Established in 1928, Fujita happens to be among the antique sake shops in Tokyo. If you are in the Kanda neighborhood, you may find the place to be rather modest at first, but do not be fooled by its humble appearance. Once you are to step in, you will be overwhelmed with the nostalgic retro ambiance of the spacious bar that has been owned by a local couple. While they only offer three unique cocktails at the bar, you can pair them up with their scrumptious appetizers. Whatever you order, you are bound to get a true taste of Tokyo, varying only according to the season.

Kimijimaya

Located near Ebisu Station, Kimijimaya is one of Japan's prestigious heirlooms ever since it was first established in Yokohama in 892. Given years' worth of experience, the place is bound to leave you exclaiming, 'Wow!' What makes Kimijimaya a spellbound place is its nature. It is a Kaku-Uchi, a solo bar within liquor stores in Japan, offering visitors an inexpensive sampling place. To provide the customers with the best of choices, the president of Kimijimaya personally goes down to breweries and hand-picks their best sake.

One thing I love about this place is that it revises its menu on a daily basis. No single day at Kimijimaya is ever dull. I would recommend tourists wanting to try sake for the first time to visit Kimijimaya. Not only will you get to sample a different sake daily, but it also offers food pairing samples. With the simple feast sampling it offers, there is no way you will be spending your money wrongly here.

Bar Gats

One of the misconceptions that most foreigners have is for sake to be consumed warm. While not entirely true, some sakes are meant to be served hot. But be warned, only an expert can truly do this the right way, to heat the right sake at the right temperature, else you will be in for a bitter experience.

At Bar Gats, while your bartender will not let you have a say in the sake being served, you can opt out of the three variants – Nurukan (40°C degrees), Jokan (45°C degrees), and Atsukan (50°C degrees). While you will not face difficulty in the choices since Bar Gats has no menu, you may face difficulty in finding a place since the nature of this bar is rather cozy. It can only accommodate eight people at a time.

Kuri

If you want to indulge in a mundane and traditional experience of sake drinking, then Kuri, situated near Ginza station, is the place for you. After work hours, the bar is flocked with office workers who are blowing the steam over a glass of sake. What makes this place distinct among its competitors and the reason that attributes to sake sommeliers swooning is their selection. The owner happens to be a fussy fellow who never repeats a sake twice, at least not in a long time.

To offer the consumers with a sublime experience, the owner only keeps one bottle of each type. Not only does this ensure that we are served with the highest quality, but it also allows us to make a glorious selection. The magic of this place does not end here. The bar is equipped with staff meant to accommodate your needs and help you select the right sake.

Akaonai

If you are tempted to try a unique, mature, or aged sake, then Akaonai is the spot for you. Finding the place is a hunt in itself, making your experience there tenfold more exciting. Once you manage to weave a path for yourself from the maze of Sangen-Jaya station, you will be rewarded heftily. The fact that like the competitors, it also rotates its menu adds on to the hype of the place within locals. To think that it rotates its menu of vintage and rare sakes continuously, the venue is a treat in itself. Now its name may translate into Red Devil. Do not be fooled by it. The ambiance, the staff, and the variety of sake that comes with appetizers only lead to an enriching experience.

Tokyo happens to be a favorite destination among locals and tourists for good reasons. It is a city that offers you the best of both worlds. From local delicacies and delights to the trending ones from elsewhere, Tokyo serves it all. Even if sake is not highly raved in Tokyo, you will be surprised to find hidden venues within the city. As you will embark on the journey to discover sake, you will come to realize that your vacation could easily turn into a more rewarding experience – one of treasure and treat.

Sake brewery tour and tasting in Osaka

You can go on a tour with a sake tasting right in the century old breweries around Osaka and some of them are located near the airport.

Kitashoji Sake Brewery

Kitashoji Sake Brewery is located near Kansai International Airport. You must book your tour and tasting one week prior to your visit. This brewery makes the "Shono no Sato" brand.

Daimon Brewery

Daimon Brewery is in northeastern Osaka near Kyoto. Rikyubai is their famed brand that has a gentle aroma and simple taste.The tours and tasting is available in English. Daimon also runs a restaurant and bar at the brewery named Mukune Tei. The setting is both rustic and quaint. It's a great treat to drink sake where it is brewed.

Isaka Brewery

Isaka Brewery is also located near Kansai International Airport. Tours are available on Thursdays, Fridays and Saturdays from 1:00 pm to 4:00 pm, and are free to attend with a prior booking that must be made through a travel agent.

Saijo Limited Partnership

The brewery of Saijo Limited Partnership, was established in 1718. The famous brand Amanozake has a Junmai daiginjo undiluted sake that has a fruity and mellow flavor. The tour is available on Saturdays in February and March.

Yamano Shuzo

Yamano Shuzo (brewery) is located in Katano, between Osaka, Kyoto, and Nara. It is a small sake brewery. They have inherited the traditional brewing from the end of the Edo period. The 80% of products are the specially designed sake, and the 40% of them are "Genshu" undiluted sake.

Tours are free, but reservations are required. Yamano Brewery is closed on Sundays, public holidays, and Saturdays from April to October.

Shimada Shoten

If you have no time visiting the breweries in Osaka, this local shop is well worth tracking down. It's a shop but has an underground level cellar filled with sake bottles of varying quality and size. For one hour, you can try any sake at $2 per glass. No reservation is needed so you can just walk in.

Sake brewery tour in Nada

The famed sake breweries are mostly located in Uozaki-go, Mikage-go, and Nishi-go that are three of the five villages of Nada in Kobe City (near Kyoto and Osaka).

The Hakutsuru Sake Brewery Museum

You can start your day trip from Kyoto and Osaka by visiting the Hakutsuru sake brewery museum that is constructed in one of its old brewery buildings. They have a tour. If you have time for only one place, this would be it. The gift shop has a wide variety of sake and sake cups.
4-5-5 Sumiyoshi Minami-machi, Higashi Nada-ku, Kobe
TEL: 078-822-8907
Open daily 9:30 – 4:30, closed Mondays.

Sake brewery tour in Fushimi

In Fushimi, there are about 40 sake breweries and are densely located in one tight neighborhood like Napa and Sonoma. It's worth a walk-through.

Gekkeikan Okura Memorial Hall

Gekkeikan's Okura Memorial Hall sake museum is by far the most worthy of a visit. It's one of the oldest breweries in Fushimi. The tour includes a partially viewable mini-kura. You can also enjoy a sake flight that includes three sake from the breweries in Fushimi at Fushimi Yume Hyakushu Cafe near this museum.
Phone: 075-623-2056 Open 9:00 – 16:30 Closed Mondays

Challenge of sake in Tokyo

There were a few sake spots in Tokyo adored by locals, yet the stores face a sour fate. With more winery options being available, the younger generation seems to be deviating from this culture. This is posing a drastic threat to the existence of sake. By 1945 when WWII ended, many breweries had already run out of business. On top of that, more and more people opted for whiskey, wine, and beer. Sake continues to be at a disadvantage. The people of Tokyo became somewhat reluctant to accept their own cultural heritage. To them, beer is more appealing when hanging out with friends, and wine seems like the best option when celebrating something.

After all, there were etiquettes to drinking sake, and the western culture does not bind a person to any customary way to consume a drink. With the temperament and nature of Tokyo, foreigners find it shocking when they do not find sake at every crook and corner. I mean, until a few years back, even Nihonshu was not widely available in Tokyo. The reason is simple – it is not a Tokyo drink. The outlook Tokyo has of Nihonshu is that the beverage is unrefined and meant for older men. Such a perception is not limited to only Nihonshu but sake in general. The younger generation is simply moving away from its roots, wanting to explore more of what the world has to offer than to be divulging in the offerings of their own.

Satoko Ustugi sake tour

With the heritage of sake in decline, one sake devotee has taken it upon herself to prolong the lineage of this cultural-rich drink as far as possible. Satoko Ustugi, a sake sommelier, is renowned for taking tourists visiting Tokyo on an enthralling experience of tasting sake. From briefing them about Japanese history and culture to highlighting some of the places that serve the best sake in town, she does it all.

She takes sake, for example, before beginning her tour, showcasing the wide spectrum available in bars all over Tokyo. Her tour is well-acclaimed for its adventurous aspect. She not only educates tourists on sake but also hands them a light of quest to find the best sake, which takes the tourist through the city. So they end up killing two birds with one stone. Satoko, like most of the young Japanese, was not always interested in sake. It was only in her 20s when she discovered sake. She had been swift to identify how westernization had altered the outlook of sake. It was being perceived as an outdated drink. She believed sake needed to be revived, much like how breweries have been doing over the decade by offering different cocktails and brews. Her tours are fascinating.

She sits with her tourists and begins by sharing the basics with them. Her interactive questions let her guests feel a part of the introduction, so it is not a boring classroom sharing. From what sake means to the brewing process, she ensures that all of the guests know where the drink comes from that is available back at their home-markets as well. This is what I have learned myself.

If you are to understand something from the very start, you are better equipped to grasp further knowledge and feel a sense of pride when you consume that product. One thing that always concerns me about sake is the label. All inscriptions on it are always in Japanese, which obstructs a person from purchasing it. Honestly, no one is comfortable purchasing a product they know little about and cannot comprehend the guide. To tackle this issue, Satoko brings a label of the bottle for her group and carefully begins to dissect it. From the number percentage that refers to the polished rice to the type of sake and the meaning behind the name itself, everything is laid open for the tourist to take in.

Now comes my favorite part. Satoko is one to realize that giving away all of the information is overwhelming, hence each time she shares a piece of information, she explains the reason why. For example, the type of water used in sake. The reason for the rice having been milled at a certain percentage and how it contributes to the overall texture. The more she shares, the more the tourists understand sake and are able to decide which assortment they are most attracted to.

Naturally, the tourists ask her questions. Questions as to what makes the drink sharper, the optimum temperature, and how it affects the quality and taste of the sake. While I have shared the information in previous chapters for you, you can determine it yourself that the information may be swamping when told in one class. So Satoko keeps it simple. She explains, if rice is polished less, it gives a more earthy tone with a stinging after the effect of the alcohol. These are the kind that can be served warm.

Now, if the tourists here taste a sake that stings their throat, they will know that not only the rice was less polished, but they should also be consuming it warm. Even the kind of water used has an effect on the drink, especially for Nihonshu. If soft water (Nansui) is used, the sake would have a subtle taste. If hard water (Kosui) is used, the results would be of a stronger, earthier, and mineral-ish taste.

Most of the tourists who may have done a little homework beforehand are quick to question why all sakes are not served warm when they are supposed to be. This is just a preference that has gained widespread attention. Satoko shares the same in her tours. Not all sake is to be drunk warm. Some are to be served chill for the best taste. Per se, if you are to consume a melon Nihonshu, the texture is smooth and does not require to be heated. Still, if you heat it, its gentle taste will be muted out.

With the ongoing class as more and more information is shared, Satoko suggests the best kind for beginners to start from. Naturally, one should not be opting for the strongest, and the complex one as the beginner should be taken aback. You should always start with a subtle and gentle sake that offers a cleaner and simpler taste. Once you understand the basic taste of sake, you can move on to more complex and versatile profiles and cocktails of sake. Unlike the olden taste, now craft sakes exist alongside many others. Some that are famous among Satoko's group of tourists are Karakuchi (dry) sake, sparkling sake, flavored sake, Amakuchi (sweet) sake, and many more. There is even a sweet-potato Shochu, which she recommends to be consumed with either dried fish or oden. This is not where it all stops. It seems even breweries have come to realize that people want more and more innovative assortments. With time as people crave for adventure, they seek adventure with edibles as well, and sake is the best deal maker in Japan. If you are on tour and express your wish to explore sake, you will be befriending a great number of people along your journey.

Satoko's approach is to take one step at a time. One step with the basic and climbing the ladder to the more complex terminologies of sake. At the end of the tour, each guest is left in awe and with the desire to find sake in the city on their own. She leaves the guest with a hope to discover something unique of their own, for them to make the most of their time there. Tokyo is brimming with places that are open to new explorers and existing fanatics of sake. Festivals like the Craft Sake week in spring, or the Japanese Sake fair held in June are some of the major tourist attractions as well.

Chapter 12
Sake: Global Expansion

Prediction of sake's future

It is no surprise how rapidly sake has established a fandom globally for itself. Even when locals have started to deviate from their own product, the overseas market for sake is only getting started. Sake is no ordinary drink, after all. All the effort that goes in and the precision required to make a batch of sake deserves more than just recognition and appreciation anyway. This appreciation is evident in the hike in exports. I can certainly vouch for this from my experience at Burning Man. My sake bar was a hit among the sea of foreigners. Even those who were tasting sake for the first time were coming back for more and more.

Sake is a centuries-old drink, and I do not see it fading away any time soon. In spite of locals moving on from the rice wine produced with care and delicacy, if you are to google the sake export report published by the Japan Brewery Association Central Association, you will be amazed to find the record is at an all-time high within the last nine years. Do you know what that means? Yes, the sales surpassed all expectations by crossing $200 million worth of sales for the first time in Japan. Have a look at the graph below by Financial Province Trade. You can see the boost in sales for yourself.

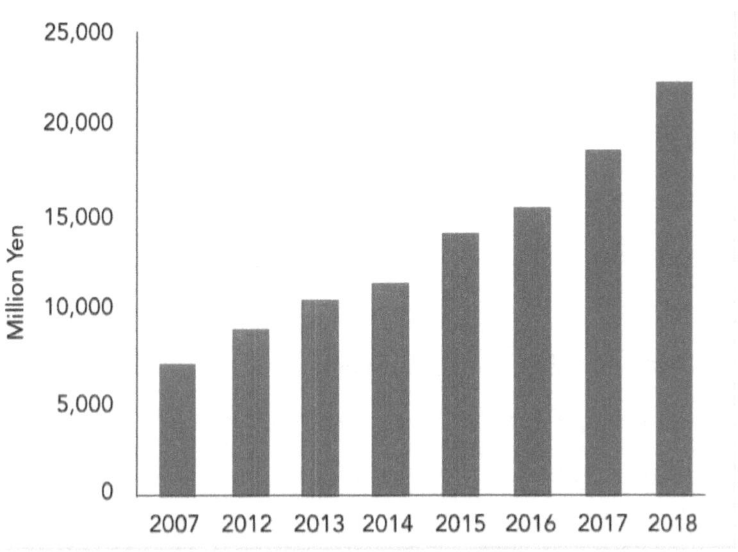

Percentages of Tokutei-Meisho-Shu (Premium Sake) Exported from Japan

2005	2006	2007	2008	2009	2010	2011	2012	2013	2014	2015	2016	2017	2018	2019
26%	25%	26%	26%	26%	26%	27%	26%	27%	28%	30%	31%	33%	34%	34%

The total exports crossed an amount of 22, 223, 1,507,000 Yen in 2018 alone. This meant the world consumed nearly 25,746,831 liters of sake, which is three times the amount that was consumed just a decade ago. It fills me with pride knowing how people are admiring sake, as once it was a staple in Japan. Now the U.S. seems to be taking the lead in appreciating sake. Not only do they love sake, but they are also the leading importers and exporters of Japanese sake. The sales from the U.S. alone were $6.3 billion, China coming next with an increase of 35%, a promising export growth rate. The amount they consumed is unbelievable, but if you taste sake once, you are guaranteed to be hooked to the taste.

At the same time, if we are to look at the local sales, they have only been dropping. Perceptions have only changed with time, and as mentioned previously, and the newer generation's vision and taste do not align with the older ones. Breweries, who were at risk of closing due to this perception, finally figured out how to break the taboo regarding sake. It was reinvention. I came to realize the real deal-breaker for the Japanese population. What truly led to the downfall of sake was not the beverage itself, but the craving for something new within the people. It was more about the quality than the quantity.

The graph below clearly depicts the turmoil faced by sake in Japan. The sales were falling and rising over the years in terms of quantity.

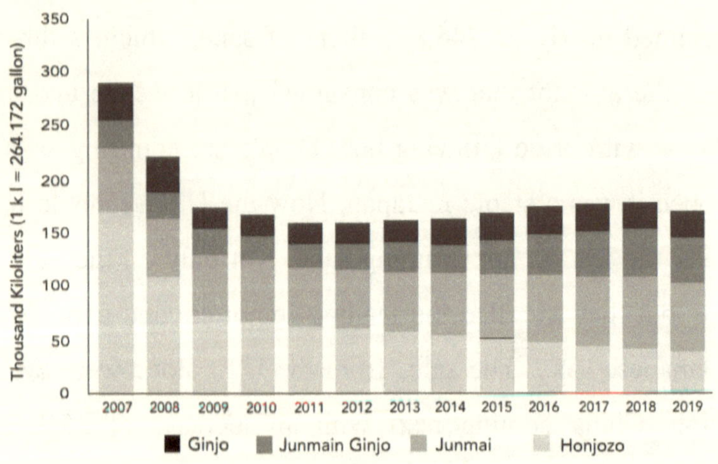

Above is a graph stating the statistics of premium sake in terms of domestic shipments for the years 2009-2019. In the year 2018, nearly 71 countries exported sake. The numbers ever since keep multiplying. Out of these, 80% of the sales were solely from five countries – the U.S., South Korea, Taiwan, China, and Hong Kong. The price that was prefixed at 863 Yen per liter, excluding Hong Kong, was 1,800 Yen per liter, and in the U.S., it was 1,061 Yen per liter. These were the above-average pricing, while Taiwan and Korea's export pricing was below average.

Even the exports for Dassai increased by 300% as more and more people overseas acquired the taste for premium sake. Previously, sake brewing was restricted to Japan. Meaning, it was to balance out excessive competition within the industry while elevating the export sales and stabilizing tax revenues generated.

This regulation is to be overturned within the first quarter of 2020 by the Japanese Liberal Democratic Party. Now the government will be allowing licenses for more breweries and for exports specifically. Sake market had been pretty dry locally, due to which, as per the Japanese liquor tax law, brewers had to produce a minimum of 60,000 liters a year, hindering newcomers in the market.

The appreciation sake received recently has forced the government to revise its regulations. This means more sake for people who do not reside in Japan, but doesn't this not make you wonder what contributed to such fanfare of sake and sky-rocketing sales? The answer is simple. Someone must have raved about sake to their friend's circle outside. Someone must have visited Japan and brought back a piece with them, introducing it to their world, and then that world would be falling head over heels for sake.

Sommeliers leading sake around the world
Surely, the sales of sake must have been done at a larger scale. It must have been introduced by sommeliers. These are the true devotees who not only understand their brews, but they are also able to dissect each bit and present it before you. These sommeliers are the geniuses behind the widespread use of sake and Japanese cuisine. Over the years, the world has come to cherish sake.It is these sommeliers we fans owe our loyalty to.

One of the examples of sommeliers making the world go around is their presence at the Ozawa Shuzo Brewery. The buzz with exhilarating energy as trucks after trucks are loaded. Each truck filled with towering boxes containing sake. These bottles then embark on a journey to new lands – Thailand, Vietnam, South Korea, the U.S., France, and Singapore, where the bottles are uncapped, and are poured out for indulgence. After commemorating such a tiring journey, the bottles finally reach our grip as more and more as manufacturers are opting to import their sake, since demands back at home are still in a slump. The role of a sommelier does not end here. With great demand, comes an even greater thirst for knowledge. People want to be fascinated by the unwinding magic that takes place under the craftsmanship of a Toji. Ozawa Shuzo embraces the swarming tourists heading over to its brewery.

Junichiro Ozawa, the president of the 300-year-old brewery, is not the only one to have taken this approach. More breweries in Japan have opened their doors to consumers to let them be a part of the process. The more people come and observe the sacred practice, and they come to understand, respect, and admire the brewing process.

Not only this, as the breweries open their doors, they offer samples of their flavorsome brews. Even the alluring and affluent wine advocate, Robert Parker, shared his opinion of sake through his rating on the beverage, drawing in more people to explore the world of sake. In the sea of sake admirers, the United States happens to make one-quarter of the total importers of sake. In a decade, we have witnessed the sake sale doubling and tripling up to 18,180 kilo-liters. As the Japanese government is impressed by the increasing numbers, it still believes there is ample room for growth and market expansion.

Since shipments take less time to hit the markets of China, sales over there have blossomed three-fold since 2008 and two-fold in South Korea. As for Hong Kong, while sake takes longer to reach their shores, the fanatics over there compensate by ensuring that sake is offered on more and more menu cards of restaurants all across Hong Kong. Be it an upscale town or downtown, you can find sake readily in continental restaurants. People just have taken sake to be the ideal pairing with their food or to simply unwind with their friends.

Breweries and the government have come to realize the power of sake. It can bewitch hearts, enhance friendship, boost mood, among other things. The authorities are using this to their advantage, displaying another side of Japan to the world apart from Anime and Sushi. Do you believe if I tell you there are at least 89,000 Japanese restaurants in the world? This was just the estimate from 2015. From 55,000 in 2013 to 89,000 over the next two years, I cannot think how rapidly the number of restaurants has increased. To strengthen the bond between Japan and the U.S., Prime Minister Shinzo Abe presented President Barack Obama with sake brews native to his region. Prime Minister Shinzo Abe repeated the gesture of friendship with Russian President, Vladimir Putin. It was a practice long observed in Japan. As a symbolic gesture of wanting to extend friendship toward someone, people would present one another with bottles of sake.

If we are to take a moment and recall the history of sake,

it was a drink signifying festivities and joy. It was used in the commemoration of holy rituals, festivals, and other occasions. Even gatherings would be incomplete without sake. People believed the drink to entail powers that would eradicate all negative vibes and evil spirits. Alas, the rave of sake started to simmer down as people grew bored by the concoctions. The younger generation drifted toward the sturdier notes of whisky and the elegance of the wine. While the consumption first hit the level of 746,000 kilo-liters, it drastically dropped to 557,000 kilo-liters over the course of ten years. Sake was no longer 'trendy' as per the young adults. Now the older generation has limited its consumption simply for health reasons. They do not wish to challenge their liver and consume sake in a limited amount. Sake's popularity is drowning, and the ones trying to rescue it are the sake sommeliers. Who better to validate this verdict than the President of the Sake Service Institute International? Haruyuki Hioki shares that as he trains over 1000 of sake sommeliers, they are equipped with enough knowledge about sake to be educating others elsewhere.

People tend to be hesitant when trying new things. Even if you are to go to a restaurant, would you order a dish without knowing what goes into it? No, right? Such is the same for sake. When people get to know how simple the drink is, they are intrigued by it and give it a try.

Within the U.S. alone in the first quarter of 2019, the sales from sake were so overwhelming that the Japanese Food Overseas Promotion Center (JFOODO) held a meeting. JFOODO is located within the southern part of the U.S. During the meeting held between the Southern American Sake Association and JFOODO, it was revealed that the sales generated from sake alone equated to over $1M. They were taken aback by the results, the meeting adjourned with a vow to have the sales soar up to $2M. This was not all. There was a sake tasting experience held in Las Vegas in May 2018. The people were flocking over sake tasting and encountered a rare convention composed by a gathering of wholesalers (WSWA). Now, because the conference caught this chance, a business deal worth around $1.5M was shaped.

Apart from the United States, initiatives are even taken in China by sake sommeliers. The first Asian International Sake Contest (Sake China 2018) was held in August 2018 in Beijing. The development of sake there was surprising. A challenge was held in which 800 general purchasers explored 137 genuine sakes and chose winning sakes that suited the flavors of China. Likewise, in January 2019, utilizing the honor-winning sake, a team with the Ministry of Foreign Affairs' Nearby Attractive Overseas Transmission Project, held a tasting occasion on January 17,

2019, receiving an honor at a Japanese strip mall.

If people were finding the marketing pattern of sake through associations, the Japanese took a rather creative way of promoting sake. Japanese sake was set on a journey from Kyushu to Shanghai from February to March 2019. Japanese shops offered sake, pressed rice, rice saltines, and tasting along three voyage dispatches through the arrival course from Hakata and Nagasaki. promised, for example, that sake would be sold out on the day after the tasting and the following day. The business volume during the period was 180 boxes.

You see, sake sommeliers are not just brewers who have a passion for their produce, these people are educators. They are the heritage, wanting to share their culture and lineage with the rest of the world. Their efforts have been fruitful thus far and will continue to bring sake in the limelight that it truly deserves.

Viability of Sake's Global Expansion

Sake has come so far from fighting a battle of survival within Japan, to floating astray and reaching the bays of other ports around the globe. This is just the beginning of sake reign. Where there is a road of opportunities, there comes a crossroad of self-doubt. Will sake continue to strive or face another decline? The answer to this predicament lies in all the products available worldwide. Japanese cuisine has been quick to gain fame internationally, including sake to such an extent that Nestle has planned a twist as well. We all are already lusting after interesting assortments of Kit Kat that come from Japan.

Well, Nestle will be adding another flavor to their collection – sake Kit Kat. The reason behind this, brewers have suffered losses in their hometown and turned to markets abroad. Due to their willingness to sell their products on a wider platform over the years, we now commonly hear of trade fairs, conventions, exhibitions, and competitions for sake and sake sommeliers.

One such sake that has acquired a prestige platform and is available on the wine card at ritzy Paris restaurants is the Kamoshibito Kuheji. It is the sake from the Banjo Jozo brewery in Nagoya that is specially crafted for overseas consumption. With over a dozen workers in the brewery, Banjo Jozo once even resorted to mechanized means of production just to meet the demands of their customers. However, as they soon realized their quality was drastically affected, they decided to compromise on quantity but not quality, which earned them the reputation and honor they have. Accordingly, Banjo Jozo's sake production volume has dived to a fifth of their original production level over the past 25 years. Instead of trying to build volume, Kuno strived to never let quality suffer because of demand. It was that devotion that earned the company its stature it has today. Kuno headed out to other business sectors to sell their products. Bit by bit, he picked up clients in Germany and Switzerland, and France. His hard work, patience, and his unwavering determination to succeed are just some of the key ingredients that resulted in the growth of the company and contributed to the growth of sake.

Kuno is evidently offering sake for outside customers as Japan's response to wine. He wants to show to the world that sake is blended just the same as wine. He just believes that sake needs to be brought further and further until it receives the same attention and appreciation as wine. The volume of Japanese sake in financial terms in the year 2011 totaled around 600,000 kiloliters, more than what it was in monetary terms in 1996, concurring with the National Tax Agency, which is answerable for directing offers of mixed beverages. In the meantime, the volume of fares has continued to develop, coming to around 14,000 kilo-liters in 2012 as per the statistics provided by the government. Now and again, a frantic move is attempted by the sake brewers who are pushing to thrive as a result of the decline in sake sales in Japan. Still, it is surprising as the government is finally taking initiatives to help the local sake industry overcome the setbacks within the global market. A few brewers are forcefully seeking remote clients.

Isojiman Shuzo, a sake brewer in Yaizu, flaunts such vigorous household requests that he is unable to make enough sake to fulfill the hunger. You see, the more a brewer injects efforts in terms of quality, the more their customers are thirsty for their brew. It gets harder to meet the ever-growing demand.

Sakata Shuzo in Sakata is investigating business openings in Asian nations in France and Belgium. He is just another devoted brewer who is offering a wholesome brew. Seeing the success of his competitors, he does not believe in giving up.

Another name promising us the glory of sake is Shoichi Sato, the leader of Sakata Shuzo. He wishes to promote sake as a visage of Japanese culture to increase boundless acknowledgement. He understands such a power move will require a handsome investment, but he is certain that it will be acknowledged, given he puts forth tolerant attempts. Patience is surely his virtue.

The sake has opened up a new chapter with more people universally acclaimed for it. As the demand for sake grows, there comes a need for universal regulation of sake.

The more quantity will be sold, the more revenue it will generate. Furthermore, useful projects are planned for showcasing the sake in the U.S., which will establish an expansion in the sake promotion within North America.

With all the efforts being put in, I firmly believe sake is viable for expansion around the world.

Where is sake going from here?

Is it not just a drink that can be dated back to 500 B.C., but sake has evolved and become a new type of wine for many. This is why it does not surprise me that the growth in sake sales has been rapidly growing. Nonetheless, as the demand prospered, it blossomed an opportunity for sommeliers and sake fanatics to expand their expertise. Today, breweries are standing tall and functioning to meet the ever-growing demands of the consumers everywhere. Breweries opened one after another.

The international fame of sake resurrected its dying fandom in Japan. In my opinion, the true reason sake lost its fandom in Japan is the low quality sake produced with distilled spirit to fasten the production and lessen the usage of rice.

Junmai pure rice sake by Fukumusume Sake Brewery in Nada Ward, Kobe City, contains distilled alcohol and was discovered in 2013. While there is nothing wrong with adding distilled alcohol, the problem arose due to the label having been claimed as pure rice sake. Upon further investigation, the company acknowledged having been doing so for more than four years discreetly. Ever since, more of such cases sprung to notice within the same year.

Namana Sake Brewery in Hannan City came forward in February, followed by Osaka prefecture, Nisshinshu in Kamiita Town, Tokushima prefecture, and Yoro Sake Brewery in Yamanashi City. Companies seemed to have resorted to this measure despite the price of sake rising, in spite of the cost of rice declining.

Is brewed liquor the same as a liqueur? No. Because it is seven times the tax rate. Under the U.S. liquor tax law, liquor with brewed alcohol is not classified as Japanese sake but as a mixed concoction with a high tax rate.

According to the Japan External Trade Organization (JETRO), the U.S. federal liquor tax divides alcoholic beverages into three broad categories. (1) beer (2) wine (3) spirits. Sake without brewed alcohol (Junmai sake, Junmai Ginjo sake, Junmai Daiginjo sake) is treated the same as beer. Thus, it is treated as distilled spirits. The same sake, but with the addition of another alcohol, is considered a mixed sake. For example, a case of sake with an alcohol content of 15% is a pure rice type, costing $0.58065 per gallon (3.7854 liters). That is $4.05 for brewing alcohol, concluding the cost to be about seven times. What happens if this is wine? The cost would be $14.07 per gallon for less than 14% alcohol and $1.57 for more than 14% and less than 21%.

Under the current U.S. tax system, the export of brewed

alcoholic beverages is effectively difficult. For this reason, most of the rice market is pure rice. While the Japanese sake industry wants to export savory Ginjo Sake, there is a dilemma that the Americans are finding value in the sound of pure rice. On the other hand, port wines with the addition of different alcohols are also classified as wines. Port wine is a wine with more alcohol. However, it is not a mixed liquor but a wine. Some people in the sake industry say this classification is unfair.

Sake Sales in Numbers

The United Nations Educational, Scientific, and Cultural Organization (UNESCO) now recognizes Japanese cuisine and cultural heritage to be unchangeable as the world is developing a keen interest in sake, including UNESCO. As the world is developing an interest in sake, their interest is also stirring the remodeling of the drink.

Let's take a brief look at the year 2010 alone when the sake sales reached the lines of 8.5 billion yen. In 2015, it had escalated to 14 billion yen. The significant and promising turnover is enough to depict the demand and immense growth opportunity for the sake industry. I mean, look at the figures. 14 billion yen means a 122% increase, which means the volume of sake exported was 18,180 kiloliters.

Out of this huge number, about five million yen worth of sake was solely exported by the U.S. Next in line was Hong Kong, having exported sake worth 2,282 billion yen, then South Korea having exported worth 1,364 billion yen, China worth 1,173 billion yen, Taiwan worth 890 billion yen, Singapore worth 526 billion yen, Canada worth 345 billion yen, Australia worth 310 billion yen, U.K. worth 260 billion yen, and Vietnam coming last having exported sake worth 248 billion yen. It seemed the U.S. won the title of being a sake fanatic. However, China promises to take over that title soon.

Reflecting on the figure earned by exports solely to the U.S. worth 7.35 billion yen in 2018, the estimate is to increase up to 10.47 billion yen until 2026, implying a total revenue increase by 4.84%. Sake promises to generate such an increase from only one region. Imagine what the total revenue generated would be, given the Japanese government is to consider all other regions. We can easily surmise from this that sake has developed itself a reputation from being just a Japanese rice wine. It is a culture being accepted globally. Not just within the Asia Pacific, but the increasing hype of sales from other regions has gained sake the attention of more and more countries. Even when sales of sake are dropping within Japan, the projected sale from export is promising to expand. Exports alone are not the only reason why there has been a growth in the industry. One important factor is the merger and acquisition of companies, coming together to brew a beverage that would receive the same love from Japan, as from other countries. One such company is Asahishuzo Co. Ltd.

In 2018 the company signed an agreement with the Culinary Institute of America, intending to construct a brewery in its backyard. It is such a strategic deal as the enrollment of the Culinary Institute of America will be exposed to the brewery as well, giving students the chance to grasp more than just culinary skills. Asahishuzo Co. Ltd. set an example for other countries to be coming in such great partnerships that would be beneficial to both the breweries and institutes.

Furthermore, we have discussed in the earlier chapters how companies have been responsible for bringing sake to the attention of the world. The success of sake is more than just word of mouth from tourists and locals. The local Japanese companies identified a growing demand within global markets and seized the opportunity by either creating new breweries elsewhere or producing sake specifically for export purposes. Companies like Takara Holdings Inc., Asahishuzo Co. Ltd., Hakutsuru Sake Brewing Co. Ltd., Ozeki Sake, and Kanpai London Craft Sake are only some of the examples we have covered in-depth in previous chapters. The efforts and endeavors of these companies have greatly contributed to the sake being understood and recognized.

I must applaud the efforts of these local breweries and tourists. They caught a glimpse of the Japanese culture and promoted it to great heights. These companies recognized how people were getting bored with the common assortments available. Hence, as we are familiar with the concept of craft beer, brewers invented craft sake to take over the world with the same zest.

America is taking a keen interest in the fermentation process. Existing breweries and newcomers in the market are treading the path of distillers, craft brewers, and Kombucha makers by embracing the art of artisanal sake. On the other hand, this sacred ritual of brewing sake is being adopted by incubators, some by admiring premium sakes and some by adhering to one notion – to break traditions. I am referring to the breweries defying norms and crafting sake that meet the needs of the current times. A few countries, like Brazil, Canada, Norway, and Australia, where brewers have strengthened their roots in sake brewing, are now unraveling the ritual of sake and finding ways to experiment that would not compromise on either quality or originality of sake. Sake is no longer a drink of cosmopolitan restaurants who have been importing it at high prices. The people are now willing to pay for the premium drink. Sake is a versatile drink that is consumed for its food-pairing properties as well as different cocktails.

It was not until the 2000s that sake started to swarm the markets of New York and San Francisco, boosting its sales by a whopping 8%. This percentage was acquired by the sale of various Ginjo sakes as well as Junmai. The growth continued to multiply as Manhattan witnessed an increase in Japanese restaurants, well, until the world was struck with the recession in 2008. But as the economy improved, so did the demand for Japanese cuisine. Ever since, the U.S. has been Japan's biggest importer, having imported 89% of their sake from Japan alone. The percentage was solely based on the sale of premium sake, generating a higher income and giving recognition to sake within the U.S. Understanding all of this and how brewers had a role to play in the expansion and acceptance of sake globally, brewers and bartenders must be given credit. Why do I include bartenders? Well, no one would have picked a bottle of sake from the liquor store, given all of the information printed on the label was in Japanese.

Naturally, people would be hesitant to try it out. In such a case, restaurant owners, sommeliers, and bartenders came to work together to offer cocktails and shed some insight into the drink of their customers. This greatly aided the patrons as they were aware of what they were ordering, and their expectations were in alignment with what they were served. So instead of a surprise, the customers were left delighted, and in wonderment, with the new concoction, they were being served. Restaurant-goers, over the years, have become more adventurous. They are readily open to challenges and try out newer things in the market. Sake sommeliers have been working hard day and night, just to come up with more offerings that would grip the market immediately and gain popularity. One such offering is the imitation of the wine industry. Brewers are observing how the wine industry offers a vintage selection that consumers purchase for special occasions. Such a mindset is being implied for sake as well. By retaining the vintage collections, brewers offer a range that is just as exclusive as your celebration.

Overseas, sake has a completely opposite fate as it does in Japan. From being invisible within Japan, it is being highlighted outside as a means of a campaign by the sake brewers to salvage the drink. In fact, as per the Japan sake and Shochu Makers Association, once sake gained approval, the exports reached a record-breaking sale of $220M in 2018.

There is another strange yet interesting happening around the world. We know there are sake breweries across the globe, such as the Kanpai in London, which offer locally made sake in these foreign countries. Nonetheless, as per the geographic indicator law under the U.S. agriculture's undertaking, the only sake imported from Japan can be rightfully claimed as Japanese sake. It is the same as champagne. This initiative had been great in protecting sake and securing its current standing.

On one hand, while this secures the sales of Japanese sake, it also gives leeway to craft sake being brewed in other regions. Of course, this means the popularity of craft liquor is increasing as well, making sake the leading craft alcoholic beverage amidst the increasing sales of craft beer and craft whiskey. The shift in the demand was more than 3%, whereby the sake consumption exceeded 2.3 million kilo-liters.

Now since the export-based tax generated went up to 39 billion yen, the government is lagging in furbishing sake breweries and marketing sake overseas.

I believe the reason sake continues to excel is solely the efforts of the brewers. The effort induced by the labor, the precision incorporated, and caution maintained, my prediction concludes only one thing that sake will continue to soar and reach greater heights of success.

Future of Sake

The worldwide sake market is probably going to infer a development structure that will work on expanding the number of fare exercises for sake being sold all over the world. The worldwide interest for sake is constantly expanding. The recognition picked up by this beverage has come about because of an assortment of variables, for example, the taste, variety of items, and substance of the drink.

The interest in sake and increasing trade activities related to sake all over the world will add to a higher demand for the item in the coming years. The appeal of sake from a few nations is prompting an expansion in the worldwide sake market development rate. With the declining pattern for the sake market in the Asia Pacific, the organizations working in this area have shifted their emphasis on advancing the beverage in different parts of the world. In some North American, European, and Asian countries, there is a massive extent of development for the sake market. The government and breweries are working in tandem toward venturing outward, taking measures such as special promotional projects, sake competitions, and different events that have all added to sake market development. All of this is just the beginning of sake's future. With high demand for premium items, there will be an expansion in the quantity of exports over a few nations.

One such factor that is contributing to the prospering growth of sake is the accessibility factor. When previously sake was not accessible widely in international markets, it is now a common sight in liquor stores overseas. Brewers are not only focusing on reaching more markets, but they are also striving to offer a wider range of sakes available. One such common sake that is gaining quite the attention is the Ty Ku sake (Junmai-Ginjo type). The 330 ml bottle is priced at $11.99 and an assorted variant at $20.99 for a 720 ml bottle, but what really attracts people to it, inclusive of me, is the packaging of the bottle. Apart from accessibility that is contributing to the advanced sales of sake and the wider options of flavor, packing is playing a vital role in the sales of the drink. The first thing that appeals to us as a consumer is the outlook of any item. Half of the time, we perceive a product's value by its appearance, and the same is the case for sake.

Let's continue with Ty Ku sake. Their packaging is chic and contemporary, appealing to a wider audience. Ty Ku offers two bespoke flavors that total to 50 percent of the brand's aggregate on-ground sales. The organization is still watchful for new mixtures to present. Meanwhile, Ty Ku revealed new bottles in May, incorporating slimmer vessels with contemporary lettering and pictures of stacked stones.

Packaging has always played a vital role in the sale of

sake. How would you feel if you come across an appealing object, but the instructions are in a foreign language?When you don't understand it, you will not consume it. Thus, Ty Ku sake offers user-friendly and comprehensible packaging in the hopes of encouraging more and more consumers to purchase the sake. This is an update on the previous bottles of sake that had Japanese inscriptions on it. Only flavors do not boost the sale of sake. With the changing times, consumers have a desire to be invested in the drink entirely. From the process to the packaging, all of that matters. It is safe to say that the sale of sake, whether sparkling or flavored, is expected to increase. This effort is boosting creativity, and also offering a wider availability of sake cocktails. Sake is just as versatile as wine. Now be it a celebration, a date-night, a corporate event, or a bachelorette party, people are opting for sake cocktails to be served at their events. This trend is far from nearing an end, given we will be witnessing new flavors of sake in the future. One important factor in the growth of sake has also been the educational pursuit of the drink. Sommeliers and the Japanese government are finally taking the initiative to spread the knowledge and whereabouts of sake with the world. As I have come forward to share sake's journey with you, I am certain it will leave you intrigued to try the drink out for yourself, and maybe if your interest increases, you might resort to opening your own brewery.

After all, it is not hard but requires hard work to brew sake. But it is all worth it. What I feel proud of the most is the number of visitors in Japan who are keen on learning about the Japanese culture. This cultural learning is not confined to just the history and ruling of Japan but also the lifestyle and food, composed of sake. In fact, the Japanese Sake Information Center is now being flocked by visitors, the number is overwhelming during holidays especially. It is a museum-type building offering you all details about sake. The place is also open for organizations wanting to host their events there. While they were accustomed to seeing foreign faces walk in, they have been seeing more and more Asian tourists visiting the facility as well.

The Japan Sake Information Center expects to make individuals around the globe be mindful of the charms of sake, including its history, by offering seeing, contacting, and encountering experiences. They have four main features.

Gallery

The primary thing to see is the enormous wooden tub beautified on the roof. The divider is a cutting-edge Japanese space with a picture of lacquer-ware. In plain view racks looking like a wooden mosque, trademark sake vessels from everywhere throughout the nation are shown. All of the Japanese culture at the display is for your perusal.

Two TV screens and projectors are perched in the corridor, and different video content about liquor is broadcasted. Moreover, a tablet is provided to individuals who need to learn more about sake. They can browse through the information while touring the facility.

What's more? There are crude materials for sake, genuine Shochu, Awamori, and genuine examples of koji. Likewise, utensils called paddle sticks, and half-cut troughs for sake fermenting are additionally in plain view. If it is not too much trouble, take it by hand and envision the sentiment of crushing rice. There are a lot of spots for taking photographs as well.

Concierge

The Sake Information Center in Japan contains the most recent information on sake, inclusive of facts on sake creation. The concierge there will respond to your inquiries and provide details of sake distilleries in the travel industry, different sake occasions held in different spots, and shops where you can purchase sake.

Tasting

Different kinds of sake from throughout the nation, for example, Daiginjo Sake, Junmai Ginjo Sake, Junmai Sake,

Koshu, Sparkling Sake, Kijoshu, and so on are available there. Generally, you can taste around 50 organic products for 100 yen per cup. For individuals who think it is hard to pick, they offer an assortment of sets that are somewhat more reasonable.

Events

The Sake Information Center in Japan hosts different occasions, for example, tasting occasions by brewers and courses by specialists. They plan to be a data hub where you can discover something fun whenever you want. From the Japan Sake Brewery Association Central Association to the world's biggest wine and liquor exchange fairs such as Vinexpo and ProWein, sake organizations are effectively taking measures to develop the comprehension of sake to neighborhood merchants and alcohol stores. One such example is the Bolster Desk established abroad, helping by working in areas in the U.K., France, Hong Kong, and the United States.S.A. They are continuously speeding up to adopt the most recent sake conditions and patterns.

Another example of creating awareness about sake to increase sales is the Japan Sake and Shochu Academy. The academy aims for experts to take care of sake and real Shochu abroad. They work on sharing more about sake blending patterns at cafes and eateries. Matching seminars are also held to promote and create awareness about sake. This year, it has pulled in a great deal of consideration.

Sake on Air (Podcast) is another means of creating a wider understanding of what sake is. A solid global cast that dwells on sake will reveal to you the appeal of Japanese sake. There are about 1,750 brands of sake, including Shochu, Awamori, and Hon Mirin, in Japan. These brands are working tirelessly to expand within Japan and abroad by dispersing knowledge on sake. The more awareness they create, the higher the demand for sake grows.

Conclusion

Kanpai and cheers

Junmai sake will live a long life with various health benefits under its belt, so that Honzojo (distilled alcohol-added sake) will have to give way to Junmai, taking the lead of breweries in the U.S., Europe and Asia Pacific. This way, Japan will eradicate the cheaters that produce low quality sake, which is the true cause of the sake losing attention from the nation.

This book is more than just a guide book. It is a portal that opens up a world of sake for you. I hope all that was shared leaves you wanting to catch a wave of it, and you can be a part of the enticing sake world.

Meanwhile, the Burning Man organization announced the cancellation of the event with all the other events being canceled for 2020 due to the pandemic on April 10. As of today on April 17, the shelter-in-place order has been intact for months in California. A lot of people started to bake bread from scratch by using yeast at home. Who knows, maybe after reading this book, you develop a want to embark on your own sake-brewing journey.

###

Contact me:

Subscibe to my blog at inblackrock.com

Follow me on Twitter: twitter.com/ReikoYamamto

Follow me on Facebook:
facebook.com/Reiko-Yamamoto-Author

Follow me on Instagram:
instagram.com/cyberhedz

Line:reikopacav